HANDS-ON HEART

MICHAEL WINECOFF

HANDS-ON
HEART

■

MICHAEL WINECOFF

MOONWATER PUBLICATIONS

Published by
Moonwater Publications
P.O. Box 741
Marysville, Wa 98270-0741

photo by Les Fetchko,
Typography & Design : Mike Stowell
printed in the United States of America

■

Warning / Disclaimer
The purpose of this book is entertainment. It is
sold with the understanding that the publisher and the
author are not engaged in rendering medical advice. Anyone
with a medical problem should see a physician. There are many
accredited schools teaching massage; this is not a book of massage
technique. The author and Moonwater Publications shall have
neither liability nor responsibility to any person or entity with respect
to any loss or damage caused, or alleged to be caused,
directly or indirectly by the information contained in
this book. If you do not wish to be bound by the
above, you may return this book to the
publisher for a full refund.

Preface

Hands-On Heart is offered as an informative entertainment about a curious, intriguing, and ultimately rewarding profession. Hopefully, colleagues and others who may be interested will enjoy reading about my experience, one that I'm convinced isn't far from being a typical one for many massage therapists.

Sincere thanks to clients and friends (writers and non-writers alike), who supported me by giving love, encouragement and endless editing feedback, and to Robert Calvert who provided me with space for a regular column in Massage magazine, where a few of these stories first appeared.

I've taken pains to change names, alter bodies, rearrange time, camouflage character, and fudge about in any way I could think of to insure that no one is embarrassed (or even recognized) as someone who might be coming to me for massage, or who may have been a colleague or client of mine in the past. People in this book aren't real people. Not being a diety, I can't create or reproduce real people. Any similarity to anyone living or dead, is purely coincidental.

No club mentioned is a real club and shouldn't be taken as such just because composite club elements have been gathered in such a way as to suggest a location that club members (and guests too) may see as similar to the club they frequent.

Aside from matters of technique, I've tried to include just about everything I thought would be of interest concerning the experience of being a massage therapist.

Michael Winecoff

Acknowledgements

It's amazing the number of names that appear on acknowledgement pages. How can so many people be so important to a book? Isn't the author buttering it a bit thick? Who wants to read all those names, which really mean nothing to anybody but the writer and the people who own them?

These are thoughts I've had in the past. Now I realize how many people truly contribute to making a book what it finally becomes. These stories have been fussed over and rewritten dozens of times over a 9 year span. Many people have read and given valuable commentary on these efforts more than once: Jan Pilskog, my brothers David and Steve, Sue and Graham Anderson, Arthur Thornbury, Simon Chaitowitz, Jerry Garcia, Fred Kay, Chris Nicholson, Connie and Will Niva, Rob Emery, Bill Gleason, Doug McNear, Ken Berry, Judy Larson, and Maryann West, to name a few.

Sometimes a simple sentence causes major revisions. Sometimes influence has nothing to do with words. I wish my father, who loved a good turn of phrase (and had a great sense of humor) could have seen this book. He gave me a sense of style, and he would have been proud.

PEOPLE TEND TO GET MASSAGE WHEN THEY'RE EX-PERIENCING TRAUMA. THEY SOMETIMES ARRIVE LOOKING LIKE PAPER CUT-OUT PATTERNS; WITH INKED DASH MARKS DELINEATING EXACTLY WHERE THE RADIOLOGIST IS AIMING THE X-RAYS IN ORDER TO KILL THE CANCER CELLS. SOME ARE HANDICAPPED BY MALFORMED OR AMPUTATED LIMBS. THEY COME AFTER A DEATH IN THE FAMILY, WHEN THEY'VE BEEN FIRED, LOST A LOVER OR BEEN LAID-OFF, WHEN THE DIVORCE IS FINALLY FINAL, WHEN THEY DISCOVER THEY'RE TERMINALLY ILL, OR AFTER A SURGERY. THEY COME WITH ORGAN REPLACEMENTS. THEY COME IN DIAPERS. THEY'RE YOUNG AND OLD. SOME ARE BEAUTIFUL, IN GREAT SHAPE, AND MENTALLY IMPAIRED. SOME ARE UGLY, WITH PERSONALITY AND GREAT INNER BEAUTY. WE WERE HONORED TO HAVE WORK WHICH ALLOWED US TO BRING ANYONE, WHETHER THEY WERE FAT, FAMISHED OR SORE FROM EXERTION, AN HOUR OF PEACE.

FOREWORD
BY JAY JEFFREY JONES

Without a special interest of social reference such as sport, alternative health practices or membership in a gym or health club, most of us would never imagine that our lives could be enhanced by regular and frequent massage. As Michael Winecoff points out in this unique and engaging book, we spend much of our lives famished for touch, unaware of how much our bodies and minds need concerned and careful physical contact.

The author of Hands-On Heart takes an unorthodox and frank approach to writing about his professional experiences while putting them into the context of a personal life. Through anecdotes of touch, he explores the experience of being a person paid by others to give them his touch, with the expectation of relaxation, revitalization or restoration of some measure of wounded health. As the precisely set out pattern of anecdotes and stories reveals, Michael's conviction that massage reaches through the discomforts of the body to touch the wounds of the mind is absolute.

Occasionally these tales have the flourish of a holistic Sherlock Holmes solving another case of emotional hijack or sexual bushwhack. Just as often they make fun of themselves, like a singer in a country western song who now sees the way it really was. More importantly, they let us see that unexpected prospects for human relief

CAN COME FROM A LARGELY MISUNDERSTOOD PRACTICE.

THE VERY PARTICULAR VALUE OF HANDS-ON HEART IS THE EXCEPTIONALLY COURAGEOUS APPROACH MICHAEL TAKES IN PUTTING HIMSELF AND MANY OF HIS OWN PSYCHIC WOUNDS AND SCARS ON THE TREATMENT TABLE. THIS IS AUTOBIOGRAPHICAL 'DEEP TISSUE' WORK THAT ENCOMPASSES PERSONAL STORIES OF FAMILY, WEDDINGS, DEATH, LOVE AND LOSS. THEY CUT SURGICALLY INTO THE AUTHOR'S SELF DOUBTS, ANXIOUS ASPIRATIONS AND PRIVATE INFIRMITIES.

ALTHOUGH HE HAS COMMITTED HIMSELF TO THE ART OF TOUCH WITH A CRYPTO-SPIRITUAL CONVICTION, THIS MASSAGE THERAPIST REVEALS IN NUMEROUS INSTANCES WHERE IDEALISM FAILS; THAT THOSE WHO TOUCH AND THOSE WHO ARE TOUCHED CAN BOTH BECOME INVOLVED IN UNINTENDED EXPLOITATION WHERE MATTERS OF ETHICS, MONEY, SEX AND ROLE PLAYING ARE A PART OF THE DYNAMIC.

WHAT THIS BOOK OFFERS TO NON-PROFESSIONALS IS A FASCINATING AND INTIMATE STUDY OF A REMARKABLE PROFESSION. WHAT IT MAY SHOW PROFESSIONAL PEERS IS A PLEASURE OF RECOGNITION AND A CLEAR EXPRESSION OF THE PROBLEMS, EMOTIONAL RISKS AND FINANCIAL CHALLENGES THAT EXIST FOR THOSE WHO DO THIS WORK.

MASSAGE WORK IS WORK THAT ROUTINELY PLACES ITS WORKERS INTO THE MOST INTIMATE RELATIONSHIPS MANY (WHO GIVE AND RECEIVE MASSAGE) MAY EVER HAVE BEYOND THE INTIMACY THEY SHARE WITH THEIR SEXUAL PARTNERS.

WEST YORKSHIRE, 1996

CONTENTS

BRIDAL FEATHERS

By Wednesday, I was on my way to Value Village, Lucky Penny, That's Atomic, and Ruby Montana's Pinto Pony. I had already been to the major department stores; then to the minor department stores. I was looking for a sportscoat, and hoping to find a 'vintage' buy. My niece Mary was getting married and I wanted to find something a vintage uncle with some style would wear to a wedding.

It was a day when I would have had trouble choosing between two boxes of tacks, so I chose the wrong coat and took it home. When I got home I put it on again to appraise my appearance. I suddenly knew I couldn't go anywhere in that coat. In the shop it was 'fun' and natty. Now it appeared cheap, even sleazy. I was doing a dressing dance, my worst critic mocking me in the mirror.

I went back to the minor department store with the most majestic prices and got a brand new coat. When in doubt spend a whole lot more, seems to be my motto, especially when suffering a fit of fashion insecurity.

Weddings remind me of my wedding day, which no doubt was why this one was throwing me into confusion. That day was a disaster, though the marriage lasted seven years and had its points. My ex-wife never let me buy anything pathetically ridiculous for instance, so I was at least reasonably dressed for the duration.

As I dressed for this wedding, I discovered that the salesman had neglected to remove the plastic security device from the coat. Some-

I

how it had not activated the alarm as I left the store. I didn't have time to go back to the store to have the gizmo removed, but it was attached to the inside pocket and it didn't show, so I left for the wedding with it pressing against my ribcage.

My brother's ex wife Julie, was standing outside the chapel when I arrived. The divorce had been final for three years, but my brother was a born-again Christian. It was his contention that the state had no power to dissolve a union that had been blessed by God. While this made a kind of heavenly sense, Julie was still earthbound, and could hardly call upon God to make an outcall and do the job Himself.

She was looking distressed as I approached her up the walkway to the church. A man in a Scotsman's full kilt regalia was playing a weeping and quite moving bagpipe on the lawn.

'Mary's back is really hurting her,' she said, 'Could you do something for her?'

'Of course,' I said.

My mood lifted as I followed her into the building beside the church. I was useful, I was needed, I even had my very own security device.

If I could have had an insecurity device - something electrical to emit beeps when I was a worry-wart - I might have seen the worry-prone side of myself sooner. I had my abilities of touch to hold me together in the meantime.

Mary was standing in a room with a pale green carpet. The bridesmaids, all dressed in baby blue, were standing beside her as though impatient for a train to take them somewhere wonderful. There were two flower girls with pink dresses that seemed to make the room glow.

I suddenly felt like I had walked into the ladies powder room. I even staggered slightly on the carpet to see so many virginal looking maidens all decked out in diaphanous lace, holding floral bouquets, staring with a surprised interest at my unexpected entry.

'Michael is here to help you with your back pain, honey,' Mary's mother said, and Mary stepped forward with a look of relief, giving

2

me a hug.

'Well, I, um, I guess we may as well have you lie right down on the carpet, Mary,' I said, because there were no chairs in the room and the only table was so small the flower girls would have been too big for it.

Mary hesitated, looked at one of her bridesmaids, shrugged, gave out a grin, handed over her flowers, and considered how to get down on the floor.

She was wearing a gown that had been worn by her mother and her mother's mother at their weddings. It was a floor length gown, a very pale color. Butterscotch pudding comes to mind, but there was something grey about it too, something that clearly said time and tradition.

She gathered the gown up slightly to her knees, knelt down on the floor and looked up at me.

'Can you lie on your stomach?'

She inspected the green shag carpet, which was evidently clean enough, because she then stretched out on her stomach.

Straddling her, I slowly exerted thumb pressure along her vertabrae in a descending direction. There are two ways to go on the spine. Up the spine if you want to increase energy. Down the spine if you want to decrease energy. Mary had quite enough energy in her body. So much in fact, she was all bound up. I made three slow passes down along her vertabrae, instructing her to breathe in slowly and breathe out quickly. As she breathed out I applied Shiatsu pressure with my thumbs. By the third pass, I could feel her body release as her vertabrae became more mobile. The body is built to be in alignment. The vertabrae are architecturally evolved to stack up together. Whenever you apply pressure correctly, there's apt to be a release of tension. As the muscles release, the bones come into alignment. A great deal of release can be achieved through a soft pressure that encourages a symbiotic movement.

I was getting hot, so I took off my coat and threw it on the table. It slid off the table and fell to the floor in a way which revealed the

3

white security device. The bridesmaids were looking at it.

'I really didn't steal the coat,' I said, 'They forgot to take that thing off at the store and I didn't have time to go back before coming here.'

I felt rather foolish, but because I was touching Mary and into my work, not quite idiotic enough for anxious self indulgence.

'Can you turn over on your back now, Mary?'

Mary turned over smiling. She was breathing again. She had probably been holding her breath for a month. I sat down beside her with my legs crossed and placed my palms one under her back and one over her belly. The left palm was over her low back, the right palm was over her womb. Energy began to move down between her legs and up to my palm on her back.

I was giving her time to listen rather than be caught in anticipation. Letting her feel the warmth of my palms surrounding her body. I could feel her body unwinding as her rib cage began to release the tension poor breathing had caught between her ribs. Her body was unwinding in a counter-clockwise way. As her upper back accepted oxygen, the rib cage on her right side expanded in a downward direction. As the rib cage came down, her left hip was rising slightly. I was noticing this, not trying to do anything special, when something on her dress caught my eye.

There was a faint, ancient stain on the floor length, lace gown.

Considering that the gown was now nearly sixty years old, that it had been worn by three generations of women as of today, and taking three wedding banquets into account, it shouldn't have been surprising. But looking at the stain, I suddenly remembered that Mary's grandfather had committed suicide. And that stain, completely innocent of any suicidal intentions, somehow seemed to be a marker moving through the generations. It was barely noticeable, and I would never have seen it if my nose wasn't less than a foot away, but there it was; a stain.

The stain was like a symbol of the emotional and psychological legacies that move through time with every family. Touching Mary, I

4

was connected to her mother and her mother's mother by my thoughts, my lineage and my blood. This tissue of tissue of tissue, joining tissue through touch. Touching Mary who would teach her children by touch, a touch that would be passed on until we couldn't know when.

There was a knock at the door and Mary's mother opened it. There stood the minister, in a robe of celestial silken glory. He wasn't sure whether to be confused or amused to see us there on the floor.

While Mary's mother explained who I was and what I was doing, I realized I felt finished anyway, so I got to my feet. I put on my coat and introduced myself. My new coat was also silk. But touch was as close as I would ever come to giving absolutions.

'It's time,' the minister said.

The wedding vows were extremely traditional. Honor and obey, and etc. Quite a bit of marital counseling from the man of God. Right there in front of the congregation. I guess a marriage is a moment of glory for churchmen, but they often seem to play to it a little too long and self-satisfied. Nothing like a little preaching to make us feel important.

My grandmother had died several weeks before, and after the ceremony, there were condolences. It was such a shame she couldn't see her great, great grandaughter married.

Pink punch was served in the adjoining hall. The bagpiper wandered about in his kilt, looking staunch and bright among the dark suits of the men. The ladies seemed to be in silent agreement that they were, nearly all of them, inclined to muted pastels on this particular day. I was staring at the black mouthpiece of the piper, which hung around his neck. I don't know where the bag was, but I had no doubt it was heavy. I was about to ask him where the bag was, when my brother appeared at my side.

'Mary has some back pain,' he said as I looked at him, 'do you think you could help her?'

Was this a communication problem? It struck me that my brother's ex-wife had used the same words. Was Mary's back still

5

hurting?

'Sure,' I said, and followed my brother back to the room with the green, shag carpet.

My niece was alone in the room, writing a check. She apologized for being such a nuisance. I told her I really was so glad I knew how to help. She didn't need coaxing to resume her prone position on the floor.

Now it was a problem of energy let down. Post-marital depletion. Reality resumption, check writing. This time her vertabrae immediately mobilized as I went in an ascending rather than descending direction. I only made one pass up her back with my thumbs pressing between each vertabrae on both sides of her long erector muscles.

There was a definite release in her solar plexus area when I again turned her over and surrounded her with my palms. Her tension, probably the result of having Walked The Big Walk, melted.

The door opened and in came the groom in his tuxedo, flushed with the champagne radiance of a newly married man. His outfit came complete with starched pointed, stand-up collars, so sharp, so Edwardian, it appeared they would impale his chin if he made a wrong move. My new in-law sat down on the floor beside his bride.

I was immediately aware that he wasn't sure he appreciated this proceeding. Wasn't it his job to touch his wife? He began to feed his bride strawberries from a paper plate stamped with blueberries.

'This is a wonderful day for you both,' I said.

'It's just nerves, she'll be alright,' he said.

'Of course, I said.

The groom was implying that the sooner I stopped touching his wife, the better he would feel, so I finished quickly. Mary rose with me and gave me a great big hug.

'You don't know how much this has helped,' she said.

I thought I did know. Because I was married myself on the same kind of day. I knew as her parents knew, not only the excitement and the fear, but because I had seen the divorce side of marriage, as they had.

My niece had been living at home while her parents went through the long, slow shredding of her father's marriage to her mother. By implication it was possible her own marriage might end up the same way or even worse, as had her grandmother's marriage had through suicide.

Her grandmother sat in front of me during the ceremony. I wondered what she could be thinking as she saw her grandaughter married in the dress she had worn herself so many years ago. The dress her daughter had also worn. A dress being passed from hand to hand. I even had a fancy that the dress, being worn only three times by three daughters on three of the most important days of their individual lives, had absorbed the high, momentary tensions of the women wearing them.

Had these animated women charged the inanimate lace that touched their skins during a trying time, blood to blood, body to body? Could the 'nerves' Mary experienced be transmitted to the material. Could the material carry the tension experienced by mother and grandmother back to Mary? Was it now 'nervous' wedding dress, transmitting a collective anxiety?

The day I was married, I ran my parent's car against the toll booth of the San Francisco Bay Bridge. To please my mother, I got a haircut I didn't want to get. It was the worst haircut I've ever had. I got lost while driving my mother, father and brother to my own wedding, because I didn't own a car, always took the bus, and consequently got confused on the freeway.

My younger brother said he would never get married, no matter what.

Now he has three children, two goats, three horses, a chicken coop with birds both fancy and foul, two dogs, three house cats, four exotic indoor birds and twenty odd barnyard cats.

And a wife and mother to teach the children with the daily application of a casual, caring touch.

GRAMMY'S GREENHOUSE

The warm smell of freshly baked bread. Homemade applesauce simmering on the stove. Holding hands one night when my parents were away, and I was sleeping overnight at Grandma's. My mother's father, my maternal grandfather, was also away. I must have been eight, maybe nine. We were in bed. My grandmother in her single bed and me in my grandfather's single bed, the two of us lined up nearly side by side. With so little distance between us we could hold hands. Why did they have single beds? How did the hand holding happen? My grandmother must have suggested it. Did she unplug the lamp, set it aside and move the night stand out from between the beds, so they could be pushed together? Maybe she was lonely. Maybe I was scared. Maybe we never remember so well the little bits of information that accumulate and build up and amount, after all, to a lifetime. It's just a feeling tone we remember, isn't it? A harmonic tune that means this is someone we love, someone who makes us feel this one particular way.

And where is the tune stored? In the brain, of course. But brains without bodies only exist in jars. What about muscle memory? The supposed emotions stored in our muscles that may be triggered by touch? Is there a way of hand holding we had that night that stays forever in my ring finger, my middle finger, my pinkie? Was there a tension in that hand holding? Did Gramma's engagement ring have a sharp diamond that will always be remembered by my third digit? A kind of ring finger adagio? Hardly. But maybe

8

some very particular hand holding would always be remembered by the muscles that make up the hand. Some set of circumstances so painful, singular and devastating - that the muscles will always retain it.

When I got to the hospital years later, I wasn't prepared to see my grandmother as she now was. It was a shock seeing her tied to the bed. A kind of outrage coursed through me, and I untied her. Struggled with the torn piece of sheet that restrained her right arm, and indulged myself in my rage. Later, when the day nurse told me they had tied her because she kept repeatedly removing her feeding tubes, I understood. But was she trying to remove the tubes to die? Or were they a physical annoyance she was trying to brush away, like a bug?

Since she was in a coma, she couldn't say. And maybe didn't know herself. The feeding tube was taped to her temple. Another loose tube hung above her left eye like some cruel, comic antenna. Several strands of hair were taped in under the tubes, as if it had been done carelessly. There was horror in the details; those few strands of hair, the wiggling rubber tube. Grammy's eyes are open, but she doesn't recognize me. Her eyes aren't tracking, she doesn't appear to notice when anyone enters the room. She's eighty-six, but the air that surrounds her now, is oddly girlish and innocent. Her left side is paralyzed, so it has only been necessary to tie down the right arm. After untying her, I place her hand in mine.

'Grandma, can you hear me?'

No response. No looking, no apparent hearing. A blank face, absolutely nobody home.

After a long time, I put her right hand into her paralyzed left hand, and Grammy begins to rock her joined hands back and forth with a rapid intensity. No question about the meaning of those jerking hands, rocking quickly back and forth. They signified worry and alarm. It was the gesture of a heroine in a silent movie, Black Bart standing nearby, stroking his waxed moustache. But my Gramma's face remains totally impassive, her eyes vacant and

9

glazed.

The nurse returns, and ties her up again. The doctor says she might recover in several days, several months, or maybe never. I sit with her in shock, staring at nothing. Eventually something comes into focus. It's a foot. I'm looking at Grammy's foot, which is poking out from beneath the sheet. The nurse brings me a bowl and towels when I ask if I can wash my grandmother's feet. She points out the sink and soap, before leaving the room. The mere idea of washing my grandmother's feet gives me a little of my balance back. Washing her dirty feet immediately settles me. This in spite of the fact that Grandma takes no interest in what I'm doing. Can't even seem to feel it. Or doesn't know what the feeling means. Or doesn't care. Or can't care.

I visited most often at night. I thought I might reach Grammy more easily at night, that she might accept me as a part of her dreams. I even thought I might catch her being normal, as if the whole coma thing was just an act. I bought and read a book about coma victims. I talked to her whenever I visited. I assumed she could hear me, though what part of her hearing was connected to understanding couldn't be known.

My grandmother had always maintained a stern, turn of the century dignity. She was of Scots descent, as tight as wind being squeezed through a bagpipe. She enjoyed crossword puzzles. Enjoyed them! Her dignity came from a time of Pork Pie hats, corsets, and doilies on the divan. Now she was without a concept of what dignity was. Now she was utterly exposed to strangers. It seemed as if fate had conspired to deal her the very hand that would have horrified her the most.

The hospital moved her from bed to bed. The line between sleeping and waking was erased. It was all a continuous nightmare. The blood pressure had to be checked, the IV changed. There was a screamer down the hall. The woman in the next bed had a racking cough. It sounded like she was bringing up pounds of oysters. In three weeks Grammy had five different beds in three different rooms.

10

It was musical beds, and it even confused the family. Is she better? Is that why she isn't in her bed? Is she worse? Have they moved her to the emergency ward? I was disoriented myself, and I was completely healthy.

And sweetly naive. I knew the right brain controlled the left side of the body, so I had begun to concentrate a lot of attention on massaging her right temple. Thinking, or rather hoping that my energy could move through the bones of her head and somehow activate or repair her blood-exploded brain cells. I climbed up behind her on the bed, balancing myself on the brace beams. The electric bed allowed just enough room for me when it was raised to the sitting position. It crossed my mind that a power failure might collapse the damn thing and amputate me at the waist. Still, it was the only way to get behind Grammy, and properly massage her neck and shoulders.

Nothing I did helped anyone but me.

Still, I was engaged, I was involved, I was working at the work I wanted to have. My mind went to pictures. Maybe some picture could trigger something, turn on the tap, light the light, fire up the sleeping motor neurons.

In my Grandmother's house, I poured through the old photograph albums. I took three photographs to the hospital that night. One was a picture of my Aunt Chall, Grammy's first daughter. One was a picture of my mother. And one a picture of Grammy herself, all dressed up in a greatcoat, complete with a mink hand warmer, and wearing eyeglasses. There's an orchid pinned to her lapel. She's standing on the Great Wall of China.

'See the orchid, Grammy?'

Silence.

'You were the Orchid Lady, remember?"

Grammy had a greenhouse. She had raised orchids, and gained such a reputation that most of the nurserys in her county got their orchids from her. An article had appeared in the local newspaper one year. The title of the article was The Orchid Lady.

'You don't recognize yourself? Sometimes I have the same trouble, Grammy. Say things and then wonder who in the world said that. Or fail to say things I ought to say, and hold it against myself. But what can I say? What can you hear? You disapproved of my divorce, didn't you? Well, I didn't approve of it either. It was beyond approving or disapproving. The proof was in the pudding!

'And the pudding was sour! That's why I'm talking to myself. And why not? Was it my fault my ex was bi-sexual? For years I thought she must be a lesbian. You know what bi-sexual is, Gramma? With my ex it seemed to mean non-sexual. You didn't talk about these things in your day, did you, Grammy? Not proper. Just not done. Verboten.

'But why not talk about it now. It's the perfect time. Sure, I'll just get it off my chest, and maybe you'll be shocked into response. Maybe the truth will set you free! Hey, maybe you'll wake up and say' "gee, I just never knew. What a good thing you got out of such a terrible marriage." 'But maybe that's just marriage, right Grammy? The old single beds routine. Did Grandpa snore? Was it a triple warmer thing? You wanted the quilt and he got too hot under all that down?

'No response? Well, here's the kicker. Chally was gay. Your own daughter. Gay as Goose! You must have known! How could you not know? Maybe that's why your lace was so straight. I'm not kidding! When I moved to California and lived with her, it became evident. Extremely evident! She was a lesbian alright. Nothing wrong with it, Grammy, I'm not saying that. But how could I stay married to my ex, given the circumstances. So now you know. But do you know it now?

'Do you? Am I coming through ... ?'

In a rational moment, I could not have conceived of making such confessions to my grandmother. Talk about shock! How awful. How utterly irresponsible. But it wasn't a rational moment, and it was about to get worse.

I could have been talking about the weather, about stocks and

12

bonds, about toothpaste, which Grammy no longer needed. No intelligence shined forth. Not an inkling that what I was saying was making a landing anywhere in her head. No intelligence illuminated her cloudy, olive eyes.

Staring at her, I saw a single long hair that had grown out in three weeks, just to the side of her upper lip. No doubt she had cut it back carefully for many years. Now there was no one to tend it, so that single hair, a testosterone renegade, was suddenly there for all to see, had anyone been looking. But no one was looking. The nurses were too busy, the doctors had more pressing concerns, and the family just saw the loved one they wanted to see. The dignified, clever lady who was a little tight-mouthed, but loved.

I looked more carefully at her face, and could not see the grandmother I had sipped tea with a month before. This woman was missing her teeth! Staring at her shriveled face made me cry. I began to look around the room for the teeth. I found them in the drawer next to her bed. I held them up in front of her eyes. No focus.

'Don't give up your teeth, Grammy, for God's sake! Here, let's take them back.'

Remembering how I opened my kitten's mouths to give them medicine, I gently placed my fingers on her lower jaw and pressed down. Her mouth opened, no resistance, and I shoved in the teeth. Her mouth was dry. It didn't occur to me to think of dental adhesive. I wasn't exactly rational. I just wanted to see her wearing her familiar face. Wanted her to feel her own familiar mouth; a mouth full of teeth. And maybe there would be muscle memory too, something beneficial.

Grammy moved her jaws around a little, a reflex reaction, perhaps.

'You look so much better this way, Grammy. Oh, go ahead, chew me out if you want to. I can take it. I'd much rather see you feisty, I really would.'

But Grandmother stared straight ahead. Another day in a coma.

I put my head in her lap and began weeping.

One day I was visiting when a nurse came in, saying it was time to change Grandmother's dressing gown. I got up to exit, but the nurse asked me to help turn Grammy over. As Grammy was turned, the gown she was wearing fell away, exposing her. Grandmother reached down and pulled up the sheet to cover herself. The nurse didn't seem to notice. Where had this flash of modesty come from? Were her hands 'thinking' for her? Was it simply a reflex action?

The moment haunted me, I resolved to redouble my efforts on Grammy's behalf.

And then we were given a week to find a maximum-care health facility. The hospital beds were needed by new coma victims. The best place we could find was a nightmare. To me it seemed a mausoleum. The halls were littered with near corpses in wheel-chairs, there were no voices excepting those of the staff. The pall of hopelessness in the halls was so overwhelming that it was very hard for me to bring myself to go there. And it was time to begin to give up. There was nothing more to be done, unless Grammy came to herself, and returned to us, which didn't look likely.

Her apartment had to be closed down. The furniture and pos-sessions divided among the survivors. 'Until such time, as she might recover,' my mother said.

Although Grammy was mute, she often stroked the hair on her temple. It was her hands again, the muscle memory, something familiar I suppose, so familiar it must have been reassuring. One day while looking through a book of sign language, I discovered that this gesture means "experience" in sign. It was an apt gesture for a woman of eighty six.

Trying to comprehend what was happening to her, I had looked up the word 'coma' in the dictionary. It comes from the Greek, 'koma', meaning deep sleep, and from the Latin 'coma', meaning 'hair of the head.' In astronomy, a coma is a globular, clouldlike mass around the nucleus of a comet. Looking into the derivations of the word coma made me think of the literary connections sometimes made

14

between heavenly bodies and human bodies. Astrology being the most obvious example. The final definition of coma was a coma in photography: 'a blur, caused by the spherical aberration of oblique rays of light, as they pass through a lens'.

I like to think that Grammy was passing through the life lens, a blur of her former self, a temporary aberration of light, moving into another sphere.

The last time I saw Grammy, she made a noise. It was the first noise she had made that I knew of since the stroke. She had been in the 'home' for over a year and a half. I was so startled.

'What?' I said. 'Did you say something, Grammy?'

Years later, I still think about that noise. I couldn't tell if it was an attempt at a word, and grandmother didn't repeat it. Later, I read by a man who 'mirrors' the noises of coma victims, as a way to help them emerge from a coma. That book, Coma, by Arnold Mindell, was published several years after my grandmother died.

My mother's mother was my first real massage client. I had given massage before, but Emily was the client who gave massage back to me. And she was my first important client because she seemed to desperately need touching, though she didn't know it. Touching her gave me what I needed even though it did nothing for her.

I was so discouraged by my failure to find a job in massage after being licensed, that I had given up. Given up in anger too, since I had invested no small amount of hope, time and money in my effort to launch myself as a healer. Though I could not heal her, I was, after working with her, on a healer's path. Touching my grandmother gave me back the self-esteem which allowed me to kick the 'poor me' complex that I had taken on as my own.

No one would have suggested massage as a treatment for Emily. Anti-seizure medicine and an IV drip made up the acceptable treatment of choice. But what about the living beings that came from her, the extensions of Emily, the living greenhouse that she was? The daughter who had become a mother? The children of that mother, my two brothers? For them, there was no license to touch, only helpless grieving. A stunned limbo. Sitting by the bed, attempting a few polite, empty remarks.

I was learning that healing is an attitude, rather than an accomplishment.

ORIENTAL MAXIMS

Looking back on it, it seems completely appropriate that my first career-break as a massage therapist, should begin in a bar. If it wasn't for a family history of over-indulgence, I might not have had such a "co-dependent" need to see myself as a person who had helping hands. Not to mention that one of my mentors would never have come into the bar, if not for the beer.

Every day, a Japanese man known to be a Shiatsu 'master' came into the restaurant in Seattle, where my girlfriend Maggie tended bar. One day, when the opportunity presented itself, Maggie saw an appropriate opening, and told the master about me. I had passed the state exams for licensing, but my 'career' was limited to family and friends. Koji Suzoko had five women working for him and the only male massage therapist on his staff, was quitting. Koji had Maggie tell me to come in for an interview. The timing was right, Koji and I immediately liked each other, and I was hired

On Koji's staff we worked seven hour shifts. There were three of us (Koji included) available to do massage at any given time. There was a traditional Japanese Tatami room, complete with raised platform, Soji screen doors and Tatami mats, and a conventional massage room. The massage complex existed at the rear of the Jennifer John Salon. There were nine barber chairs and as many hair stylists. There was a manicure station and a private room for facials. As far as the massage staff was concerned, the Salon was some-

something of a sweat shop, though I didn't share that view, since I was a grateful supplicant at the time, just eager to serve. I had finally found a chance to begin doing the work I loved. And I thought I had found in Koji the ideal, the almost mythical, mentor.

Koji was the undisputed headliner of his own show. His 'record' was ten massages in one day (even though his prices for 'treatments' were higher than the rest of the staff). He averaged seven clients a day. Koji was from Nagasaki, Japan, but he had been in America ten years and he spoke English very well when he wished to speak it well. With clients, he maintained a charming, clipped English, generally limiting himself to Oriental maxims, sayings and quaint bits of Japanese philosophy. This was terribly engaging, but what made him even more effective to his staff and students (as he tended to regard us), was that he let us in on the joke, and enjoyed the duplicity - if duplicity it was - very, very much.

The first day, when I found him smoking in the employee lounge, though I was sure he had a client in the Tatami room, we had this conversation:

'What happened to your client?'

'She's turning over.'

'Turning over?'

'I always leave the room to let them turn over. I take a smoke break. Makes me better for the second half.'

Koji laughs. It's a kind of amused giggle, something childlike mixed with a clever maturity; a low clacking that only rarely changes tone, and includes something musical.

'How can you smoke so much?"

'In Japan, smoking is connected to the Dragon. The smoke of the Dragon is very powerful. Eat plenty of garlic. Always macrobiotic foods. No problem with smoking. I enjoy it.'

When I saw how Koji's clients were so ready to lionize him, were so ready to accept him as an Oriental Master, I wished I weren't a wide-eyed, white, Anglo-Saxon American. And I myself was just as eager to accept him, to sit at the feet of his declarations, to inhale the Dragon smoke and turn over slowly, each pearl of wisdom.

I dreamed unlikely dreams at the time, though I imagine they're common among massage therapists fresh from graduation, eager to learn, filled with hope and naivety. I longed to discover, for instance, that my hands weren't really hands so much as magical generators, capable of producing amazing light shows; that my palms were miracles of loving transmission, with digits so fiery they could melt rings and bend spoons. I saw touch as a sensual synesthesia, an electrical exchange of skin-on-skin as personal as a poem. I often experienced through touch a sympathetic merging with a client which went beyond giving and receiving and sustained what seemed to me to be a momentary dance of souls. It was like an unspoken waltz was playing somewhere in my mind on a muted harpsichord, with sweet, kinetic aftertones that swept aside daily concerns and somehow transcended time.

At first, of course, I was extremely professional. I was the Certified Public Accountant of massage. No matter what happened, I was a robot of suitable decorum. A beautiful woman came to the table one day, and then began to come once a week. I always left the room so she could change. When I came back into the room, she was always lying on her back, and her breasts were always exposed. I was stunned by her naked beauty, but said nothing. Could say nothing. Would not have known what to say if I had even thought that saying something was possible or appropriate. The massage was always over too soon. A formal, heartfelt thank you. A slight bow. Not quite Oriental, sort of Occidental, with just a hint of an Eastern twist. Thank you so much. Come back soon.

And she did. Nipples aimed right at the ceiling. Remarkable symmetry. Lovely color. An unusual face. Unreal cheeks. Soft and resilient. A full, a very full mouth. Black hair cut in a perfect chop. A perfectly lovely chop.

Of course, the Dean of professionalism, the Dr. Doolittle of

Digits, master Koji's pupil, was trapped in a fog of denial about the intermittent sexual feelings that sometimes arose. I had, from the very first day, adopted a calm, reassuring voice. Surrounding, but never touching, her perfect orbs. Almost speechless, but courteous, controlled. Concentrating so hard on technique. The occasional erection under the table was ignored; seemed to belong to someone else, someone crude and vulgar trying to intrude. Trying to make a liar of me for much of every hour I spent with the beauty. But I was devoted to the work. Such sincerity. Such a pro. My goodness.

There was a kind of liberation in such an amazing experience, though it was so stifling. I had no boundaries. I didn't even know what a "boundary issue" was. I was a man without a map in a virgin rainforest. I was like the robot with a program he wasn't aware of. Of course, I thought I was the quintessential professional. But my talking hands told the story. Touch always tells a story; usually a short story. Where this woman was concerned, my hands were probably conveying an earnest, but sexually confused mini-series. After six weeks, the beauty heard the story my hands were telling and stopped coming. And I had learned nothing.

I might have asked the beauty to cover up, which would have established a boundary for me, and allowed an understanding to develop. The ambiance would have changed completely. Some trust might have developed. All supposing, of course, that sexual titillation wasn't what the beauty was seeking.

And what was I seeking? My intentions were pure, my attitude spotless; I wanted to be a healer.

The only mention made of boundary issues in the massage school I had attended, was made by a male instructor.

"I'm nobody's whore," he said.

Meaning, of course, that he had a definite and well-established dividing line between work and play.

After several months I began to be more comfortable with my

20

new profession. We were required to wear Kimono at work. The clients were given Kimono too, though they usually took them off when they lay down on the table or the Tatami mat. So there we were in costume. The client and the humble beginnings of a person who was finally and at last, a massage therapist. A person trying to learn how to be with people who had their clothes off.

I began to allow myself a few Oriental aphorisms. I was a white man in a Kimono. The Fortune Cookie guru. The Koji Suzoko clone. The man with talking hands and a cotton skirt, a cultural impersonator without an authentic identity of his own. Of course, I did it well, being a natural chameleon, and in spite of my desire to be like my new master, little bits of me started to creep into my sessions.

Becoming me has always been extremely difficult. There seems to be so many other people I'm trying to be. They're wittier, more brilliant, better looking. They're successful, for God's sake, and I certainly wanted success. But I could never be them as well as they could. And time after time, little bits of me would creep out. After eight or ten eons I noticed that there were actually a few people (slightly impaired people of course), who wanted to be like me. So I began to let myself out of the box. It seemed to take a millennium, and I'm still working on it. Kind of like the Hollywood actor who thinks he's a character hack, wakes up to critical acclaim for being so natural, then tries so hard to be natural he gets all phony again.

I've always had a literary mindset, and I'm given to metaphor. So I began to see myself - my massage self - as an emotional broker trading unspoken metaphors in a semi-dark room. Yeah, I liked the sound of it. Not a massage therapist, really, but a broker of honest emotions. You want to know what you're really feeling? I mean honestly? Let me adjust this knob on your elbow. My goodness, it's grief you're feeling! Son of a gun! This is powerful stuff. I must be kind of remarkable, see what I mean?

Yes indeed, the special me, come to Earth at last.

That was how it seemed sometimes. I would touch people and the emotions would break out. Like a string of wild ponies. Like hives. Not that unusual, really. Nothing to do with strange powers. Any massage therapist experiences it. Because people often do become emotional during a massage. Sometimes the sheet gets all wet from silent tears. Or some actual sobbing occurs. Because being touched - actually touched in a kind way, a way without agenda - is such a touching thing. The brain kind of goes berserk to realize how unique it is. How long its been since we've had that kind of touch, the kind of touch that too often stops when we leave our mothers.

Koji said his mother taught him massage. I don't know whether it was the truth, or whether he just said it because he knew how well it played. Maybe his mother taught him a few moves. The way he said it, you assumed she had this vast warehouse of moves she instructed him to master over many, long years. A difficult apprenticeship. Bareback wriggling in the Winter snow. Firewalking on your knees. Butterfly strokes through the pounding surf. That sort of thing. She was probably a landscape architect, or something. You couldn't count on Koji to tell you the truth. Not that he wasn't truthful; he just knew the elusive quality of truth; knew that the apparent untruth is sometimes more true than the factual truth.

Of course his mother taught him! Didn't your mother teach you? Your mother teaches touch without a textbook. Teaches you in your pain, silence, misery and grief; in every holding, loving, touching moment.

I often told stories to my clients about my own mother, who certainly offered me maximum endless, and abundant material. I had always told stories. Simple stuff. What happened to me at the hardware store for instance. The blind usher, or whatever. I began to tell stories in the massage room too, mostly personal anecdotes, sometimes something remarkable about a client who had come earlier in the day. Never mentioning any names, of course. Clients confided so much, that confidentiality was extremely important. The massage setting seemed to me to be a wonderful place to tell stories. It was such a place of understanding, melding and meeting. A place where I gave myself back to myself, and my clients gave themselves back to their bodies.

SWEEPER AND BROOM

Touching was for me, becoming a kind of self affirmation. As if my existence was sculpted by the fact that I was able to touch others. And I could no longer imagine what would happen to me if I wasn't able to continue my work.

Working with Koji, I had been introduced to the theory of energy flow in the body. And soon realized that working from the Japanese model was working backwards, since meridian flow theory was originally a Chinese discovery, one that resulted in the science of acupuncture.

I became extremely interested in body/mind literature. The books were usually published on cheap paper. They were all about esoterica; the magic of creative imagery; auras; reading auras; psychic massage; hypnotic storytelling; the chakras; the serpent; the twelve steps; the twenty four connections; cellular memory; past life regression; prognostication; the I Ching; Tarot; Tantra; meditation; Lao Tse; the Tao; the Yellow Book of China; the Tibetan Book of the Dead; Milton Erickson; Carl Jung. It was all so revealing! So mysterious!

I became, as most massage therapists tend to become, a pseudo-psychotherapist. A hands-on, half-time hypnotist. An informed dilettante, a poor man's dietician. This wasn't an overnight thing, but the information I was learning seemed to be the kind of information many clients were seeking. I don't think I went overboard on it as things go, although I applied myself to it in an almost ob-

sessional way. I was hungry to learn. I was learning. I was eager to help. I was helping. I was licensed to rub people, and I began to massage their minds. It may not even be possible to touch the body without touching the mind.

So many people become helpless when they lie down. They lie down every night to go to sleep, and going to sleep, shut down the mind. Lying down on a massage table, the tendency is the same. All our lives, lying down is almost always a positive thing. We lie down for sex, for instance, so there's a tendency there, too. And people do ask for advice when they're lying down. People who wouldn't ask the time of day standing up, are very curious about what time it is when they're on their backs. Metaphorically speaking, of course. What should I do about this mole? Do you feel that lump? Do you think it's cancerous? I've had this skin condition for several weeks. What do you think it is?

In the salon, a female client mentioned that her knee caps hurt. She said her 'patellas' had dropped too low' after an operation twelve years previously. She said she had been to see a doctor before coming to see me. The doctor had recommended several weeks bed rest. She had already been in bed a week.

This seemed pretty amazing. After twelve years, she had been prescribed two weeks in bed? These were bad knees indeed! Pathetic patellas! The worst patellas I had encountered in all my years as a knee specialist! But I resisted the urge to schedule her for knee surgery.

I asked her a few questions.

'Are you aware that the knees are metaphorically regarded as organs of surrender?'

'I've never heard that.'

'You might be in a situation where you need to surrender, for instance. In a place where giving up or backing down is appropriate. Or you could be in a situation where surrender is what you intuitively know you shouldn't do. And in the second case, if you've acted as though you do surrender, your knees might ache. In either case, your knees might give you problems. Provided of course, that the situation is grave enough in your mind that surrendering or not surrendering makes a great difference to your psychic well-being.'

My client was quiet, thinking this through.

'Or you might have a bowel problem.'

'A bowel problem?'

'Colitis can cause pain in the knees. A twisted bowel can cause pain in the knees.'

I was suddenly sad. I had no reason to be sad, so I assumed she was sad.

'Why are you so sad?' I asked.

'I am sad,' she said. 'A man I knew twelve years ago called me long distance several weeks ago to tell me he was coming to Seattle. He asked if he could see me. I'm married now, and I told him he could see me if he wanted to be my friend, but if he wanted to sweep me off my feet, he should forget it. He came, but didn't keep his promise to act as a friend. In fact he asked me to marry him. He even maintained that my husband is bad for me.'

'What happened?'

'I sent him away.'

'So he did sweep you off your feet.'

'What do you mean?'

'Well, you've been on your back in bed, haven't you?'

The fact that her knees had begun to bother her 'twelve years ago', when she was originally involved with this man, seemed too coincidental. She might have forgotten that he made her feel weak in the knees, but her knees had not forgotten.

In time I became a very close friend with this woman, a mother of two. As it turned out later, she did have a twisted colon which eventually required surgery to correct. She was a playwright, as well as a mother and housewife, and a very creative person. She was as gentle as a wet sponge, and like a sponge, took on everything.

Of course, it takes a sponge to know a sponge. I had always absorbed everyone's mood, and become accustomed to identifying whose mood I was having at any given time. OK, this one is Mom's. This one Dad's. It was good to know who I was when I wasn't being me. I just wished I was better at shutting it off when it wasn't beneficial. A dry sponge is a little harder to squeeze.

In the matter of sensitivity, I was more female than male. My father always told me I was too sensitive. Too sensitive! As if sensitivity was an impairment, like a club foot. As if sensitivity was a curse. Of course, if a curse is the topic, then women must be discussed.

There's a rumor circulating among men about women. Women, the rumor goes are more demanding than men. And never satisfied. You can't please them, no matter what you do. Maybe it's The Curse, or some as yet undiscovered X factor. Women do have children, so they're always looking for a better cave. You need a pretty good cave when you're carrying for nine months. And a big cave too, with extra rooms, in case you find yourself carrying again. Even childless women want a better cave, because the program is already written, whether a woman gives birth or not.

Most men, on the other hand, are pretty kicked back. A beer in front of the telly is just fine. The car we've got is running, isn't it? What's the problem? Just tell me what's wrong with this neighborhood? Isn't this house good enough? We can always add an extra room, can't we? You want me to ask for a raise? We're getting by, aren't we?

My colleagues in the Salon were ready for an uprising. Koji had made the mistake of hiring a former social worker, who was familiar with state law. She was organizing for a better cave.

27

50% of the massage revenues taken in went to the salon. The normal traffic for massage was two clients per shift. Out of seven hours, five were spent waiting for business. While we waited, we were expected to do the dishes and laundry created by the stylists, manicurist and the beautician, all of them busier than we were. The women were tired of this unfair situation. They called a secret meeting in a separate cave. They had looked into the legal aspects of the case, and since we were hired as independant contractors, we weren't required to do dishes and the laundry. Copies of the law were handed out, all around. We were professionals, weren't we? Would a proctologist be asked to do the dishes? A pediatrician? Is anybody on the City Council doing the laundry? Does the Governor sweep hair off the floor? Such questions constituted a compelling logic.

But I was nervous about it.

'Look, I've only been here a year. Sweeping up the hair gets me out in front of the salon clientele. I talk to them. Once in a while it gets me a client.'

'And you like doing the dishes, I suppose?'

'I don't mind it. It keeps my hands soft. It's only a few dishes. Listen, I was a house-husband for two years. Took care of a boy from the age of two to the age of five. Did all the cooking, cleaning, laundry and dishes. The sweeper kind of becomes connected to the broom, you know? The dishwasher to his suds, the dryer to his dryer.'

'So you just loved it,' Abbey said.

'It wasn't so bad. It brought out my feminine side. I probably wouldn't have gotten into massage without that experience. Doing things for other people makes me feel worthwhile.'

'Oh my God, he likes this shit,' Carol screeched.

'Co-dependant is, as co-dependant does,' said Christine.

'I suppose so,' I said, 'but aren't we all? After a year with you guys, it's pretty clear to me that all of us need our clients as much as they need us.'

'But this isn't about clients, it's about bosses. It's about people taking advantage of other people.'

'But what about Koji teaching us Shiatsu for free when he gives his seminars?'

'Sure, he teaches us, then we become his free teaching aids every time he has a seminar. I don't have time for that any-more. We're not paid for that, are we?'

'I do see your point. I just don't want to lose my job over this.'

'Nobody is going to lose their job. We'll stick together. If anybody is threatened with losing their job, we'll all quit.'

'All for one, one for all!' Christine said.

'So how do we proceed?'

'We'll write a letter. Who wants to write the letter?'

'Michael is the writer.'

'I can write, sure. I'm also the most reluctant. I'll tell you what. I'll write the letter, and we'll all sign it. In alphabetical order. That way, they won't know who to blame. I guess they can't fire us all.'

'The six Musketeers!'

'Let's organize the points we want to make ...'

The points were organized. And later I cleaned up the sen-tences, and fiddled with them until they seemed to make sense. And didn't say things that weren't intended. And finally, the letter looked good. And I went to bed.

And in the morning the letter looked bad. Gremlins had mucked it up. It had the wrong tone. The tune had changed overnight. So I massaged it again.

And again the following morning, more evidence of gremlins. So I wrote the whole thing over again. And slept the good sleep.

The following day it seemed to me my letter was obviously from a man. I attempted to make the letter over into a female form, but I was a clumsy literary cross-dresser. Now it looked adorable. It was so hard to write in a way which not only worked,

29

but looked natural. I worked on the letter until the hard parts were softer, without lacking resolution. Until the form seemed feminine, with purpose.

What I had not thought of, was the order of the alphabet. Alphabetically, I was last. And my name at the bottom of the letter was like the earth beneath the water. The fire under the wood. Not to mention that Japan is a Patriarchal society. Koji assumed at once that I was the ringleader.

I was fired.

While I burned, the Musketeers commiserated with me, but I think we were all in a slight state of shock. A few got misty eyed as I cleaned out my locker, but nobody elected to burn with me, bread and butter being awfully important in a world of checkbooks. Our agreement was only a verbal agreement, and our promised solidarity was forgotten in the face of my abrupt banishment.

My anger began to boil me. And so, burning and boiling, I told Koji I was going to sue. That firing me without notice was illegal. That it was unjust. That his loyal staff now had a cancer which would eat up the salon unless some reparation were made.

A few days later, Koji called me and arranged a secret meeting. We stood casually but stiffly in a public place, and he offered me the Japanese way. The honorable way of the pay off. Because he didn't want to see me go away mad. Because I had been loyal and done much of his marketing. Because tradition is important.

'How important is tradition?' I asked.

'In this case, Five hundred dollars.'

'I accept, with two provisos.'

'Provisos?'

'Conditions.'

'And what are the conditions?'

'That you give me a shift at the new club.'

'I cannot. I have promised it to someone else.'

30

'Un-promise it. I've worked for you without complaint. Always on time. Always covering for everyone else. We will still be working in the same city. You do not want me speaking ill of you. Firing me was unjust. I did not organize this complaint. I'm resolved in my conditions.'

'And the second condition?'

'That you write me a letter of recommendation.'

Koji had set up the massage program at the newest athletic club in the city. He had arranged it with characteristic care. Massage therapists working at the club recieved 80% of the take. Financially, it was one of the best places to work in the city. He considered the request. He had recently told me that he didn't like the club. That he would soon be quitting the club. And I knew it was because he couldn't smoke there. That he was surrounded in the club by people who were pumping iron rather than aphorisms and metaphors. That his legend meant nothing to the pumpers of iron. And what difference would it make, my being there, since he was quitting?

'OK, I will arrange it. You start work Monday'

We shook hands. He handed me a check. The whole time I was quaking in my sneakers. I couldn't believe my good fortune.

'Koji, you have taught me well. I truly like you. I'm sorry to leave this way.'

'I will miss you, too. It's this way sometimes. Nothing personal.'

YES, YES, EUREKA

It shouldn't have been a surprise to me that I had managed to pick one of the few careers, where being a man is a liability. I had never had a lot of financial success in my life, but I was hoping that would change. My only notable success had been in having a few poems, stories, and articles published. But even there, I had only been paid for one piece of fiction. I noticed that the women of *The Club* were almost always taking home bigger paychecks, though we were all equally skilled.

With Koji as the exception, I've never known a masseur to make as much money as a masseuse. Many men do well as founders of a style of touch, or instructors of an accepted technique, but a woman can usually fall into a pretty good income in massage right away, if she's an attractive woman. A woman who isn't especially attractive has a harder time of it, but a man has to be more skilled and quite charismatic too, to even do as well as the plainest of women in massage.

Our fathers don't touch us as much as our mothers, and when we seek solace as children, we run to Mom. Between men on most English-speaking continents, a hearty handshake is the thing. Hugs are suspect among many men, looked upon with all the suspicion of a Private Detective on a dangerous stake-out. We're often uncomfortable rather than happy about hugging, no matter how much we like the hugger. So most men, leery of being touched by a man who isn't their own father, want a masseuse rather than a masseur, to do the touching. Women are inclined to consider the issue of sexual safety at all times, so they also tend to avoid massage from a man..

I had a client, a longtime client of many years, who once thought I drooled on her back while giving her a massage. It was summer, I was hot and working hard, and a bead of sweat fell from my brow. It astounded me that she could even consider that the liquid she felt hit her back was drool. Did she think I was having so much fun the salivary secretions of my euphoria had been too much to contain?

If they're looking for a legitimate massage, both sexes are looking to relax, and trust is extremely important to letting go. Anyway, approximately seventy percent of humans beings looking for massage, want a female to do the touching. Which makes it difficult to do well as a man.

There are exceptions. Some women prefer male energy. Some men and women too, think females aren't strong enough to work deeply; that they have weaker hands. It isn't really true. I've had massage from women who have forced me to ask them to let up a little. Paradoxically, many big men, often can't stand much pressure. Often small, wiry women, can't get enough pressure, and always want deeper work.

So I was the wrong sex, and not handsome enough to turn any heads. I slept, like a character out of Edgar Allen Poe, with one eye open. As a boy I had been paralyzed for months on one side of my body. The trigeminal muscles around my eyes had atrophied. I couldn't completely close my left eye, and my right eye wouldn't open completely. It was a decidedly lopsided look. I saw that I would have to invent some new treatment form If I ever wanted to make a wonderful living as a massage therapist. I would have to write a brilliant book and hit the seminar circuit. Imparting amazing observations and incredible techniques to about forty people paying, say a hundred a day.

Massage used to be a laughing matter. A subject for embarrassment and blushing. The very idea of massage could make people giggle. I'm always surprised when that attitude persists, since massage has gained such professional credibility. Insurance companies in the United States will reimburse automobile accident victims for massage. Many states will pay for massage when it's needed after a Labor And Industries accident. One of my most engaging clients, an erudite man who had previously worked in a New York publishing house (but had a grade-school mentality about sex), suggested that The Complete Tongue Treatment would make a catchy title to launch my teaching career. But it really isn't funny, is it?

I decided I ought to take a workshop myself, to see how workshops were done. I knew I didn't know that much anyway, and being eager to learn, it made sense to take a seminar. I took a weekend workshop in the San Juan Islands, on the border of the United States and Canada. And found out that there were advantages to being a man in massage, after all.

There were twenty people in the workshop, and only two of us were men. Which gave me a much needed chance to polish my charisma. I could have been a goat at that workshop, and still I would have been invited into the hot tub. Waxing poetic in the hot tub, I met a woman named Annie and later we went back to her cabin and went right on waxing.

Which probably has something to do with why I became a workshop junkie. For years, there was no end to the workshops I was willing to attend. It was wonderful to periodically increase my skills and meet colleagues from other states. I had a burn to learn and it was also true that almost every time I took a workshop, I would meed another Annie. Fortunately, these diligent efforts to educate myself were a tax write-off.

Why do we give ourselves permission to really be ourselves, when we're away from home? Probably because there are seldom any consequences. Because we've decided to make this time a special time, so we're open to expansion. Having made the decision to go, and having choked up the money, we're suddenly free to tap our own powers as remarkable beings, open to a universe of possibilities. *Unfortunately, we don't seem to change much after we return to the normal set we've arranged after we come back to the barn.*

Workshops in massage involve very little work, and a great deal of play. And the wads of money people make from giving such workshops far exceed what they can make working with individual clients. Everybody knows that, but we're having so much fun, we don't give a rip. We're on vacation! The meals are provided, the food is vegetarian or macrobiotic, the salads are sensational and it's all much better than any of us eat at home. Meanwhile, we're floating in a pool with our peers! Pass the massage oil, Mollie, I'm ready to be cured!

Once again, we're the class clown! The slow one. The quick study! The genius! Mr. or Mrs. Sincere. Look, it's already time for lunch!

Most workshop are 'padded' with 'work study' participants, who haven't paid much, if anything for the workshop. Whatever the workshop may be called, the regimen seems to be the same. Nothing is done the first morning, because everybody is finding out who everybody else is. This is called 'Orientation', but there's no discount involved for talking about who you are. All workshops are also regression seminars, where everybody gets to be a kid again. There's a clubhouse atmosphere, and if you've paid your tuition, you're a member of the club. It's a huddle! There's a beach fire tonight! We're a team! Members of a one-time, exclusive fraternity! The facilitators are so glad to meet you, because you're paying them for the privilege. And nothing is done the afternoon of the last day, because it's party time! This is called 'Goodbye'.

Workshops do offer community, and most of us are hungry for community. The lack of community in our lives is like an open wound we try to heal by watching TV sitcoms about people who have a close circle of friends who spend all their time together, throwing surprise parties for one another. Maybe providing community, if only for a week or two, is worth all the money workshops usually cost.

One of my colleagues at The Club was an even bigger workshop junkie than I was, but she tended to go to the spiritual improvement seminars. I was always impressed that the language she used was not her own after these short trips taken to sit at the feet of the spiritual master of the moment. Her language had changed when she got home, but she essentially remained the same person. No matter how many workshops she took. The terminology would eventually die down, the language of yes, yes, eureka, would fade away. It was time to go home, warm the beans, toast the toast, and turn on the telly.

Until the next seminar.

PITCHING TEMPORARY TENTS

I studied Hawaiian massage at a workshop in Hawaii. Hawaiian massage may be the most sensual of all massage forms. More of the practitioner's body is used in Hawaiian massage. Full body strokes might begin at the feet and continue without interruption to the shoulders and out to the ends of the fingertips. Leaving all parts of the body feeling connected. The entire arms of the person giving the massage are used, right up to the arm pits. The body of the receiver is encircled by the body of the giver. Many strokes surround the body on the table, beginning on the back and describing circles across the belly. Or beginning on the belly, and stroking around the waist to the back, and down over the buttocks. Hawaiian massage can make you feel the freedom of childhood, and your connection to your mother, who has touched you in similar ways while giving you a bath when you were a baby. Lots of oil is used, to facilitate the glide of skin on skin, to evoke the mother memory and - in the best of Hawaiian massage - to evoke an ancestral connection. Hawaiian massage is a deluxe massage.

Once when I got a Hawaiian massage, it was too deluxe, though it was an excellent massage. Maximum enfoldment, great transitions from torso to limbs. Creative attentiveness. Artful turning of my body on the table. Sensitive pressure which went very deep in the appropriate places, giving my muscles permission to send my mind into limbo, and letting the tigers of tension sleep. There was very little talking; an atmosphere of silence and care created. Obvious presence; no wavering of intent.

The table, an adjustable massage table, was set low to the floor, thigh high to the woman giving me the massage. She was wearing thin cotton pants. Several times during the massage, her body rubbed against the inert, ulnar surface of my hands. I was completely relaxed, and had no sexual thoughts in my mind until the feel of her lower body brushing against my hand caused my body to respond sensually.

I considered saying something to alleviate my embarrassment, and to quell any discomfort she might have had about the telescoping pole under my temporary tent. But she was a nurse of many years, as well as an experienced massage therapist. Hawaiian massage, a very sensual touch, was her specialty. I knew she had seen sheets rise in the past, because I had seen a few rising sheets myself. And because she was a feminine, sensual woman, I knew that in the matter of rising sheets, she had seen more apparent levitations of cotton than I would ever see.

So I didn't say anything, and simply enjoyed the expression of my manhood while it was there, which was only a matter of minutes as she worked my left thigh and calf. And again when she came to my right side, the arousal appeared, like some grateful puppy being wagged by his tail. And went away quickly without a whimper as she finished my right leg.

The woman had always initiated hugs with me, though I had only known her a short time. We had agreed on our first meeting to do trades. The massage I was getting was the first of the agreed upon trades.

'Do you want your massage next Sunday?' I asked as she was leaving, since Sunday had seemed to fit her schedule better than any other day.

'We'll talk about it,' she said cheerfully, and we parted with apparant ease.

After the massage, I thought about the hug we had shared before she left. And it seemed to me there had been some hesitation on her part in that hug. But she seemed relaxed and at ease otherwise, so I shrugged off my thoughts. Days passed, and there was no word from her.

After a week I called, leaving a message on her answering machine. I had an extra refrigerator I wanted to get rid of. I needed the space more than I needed the fridge, and she had expressed interest. Though she had accepted the 'fridge gratefully, she had not called about when she might pick it up.

The following day, her boyfriend came to my door. He looked at the 'fridge and was enthusiastic about it, we had a short pleasant visit, and he left. Afterwards, I began to be annoyed that my new friend had not called me back, but instead had sent her boyfriend. She had never yet had a massage from me, and it seemed to me I was being slighted. Almost two weeks had gone by, yet she had not even scheduled her appointment.

As more time passed, I concluded that she must have felt uneasy about my sensual response while she gave me that first massage. Had she decided it wasn't a good idea to trade with me because of it? Was I a pervert, possibly? Possibly a jerk?

It was bothering me too much. I went directly to her house to talk to her about it. And found out that she was totally surprised that I had given it any thought at all. She was overwhelmed with worry about money. She had just moved. The press of so much change, both physical and mental, had totally preoccupied her. She assured me she had not been bothered by my arousal, and her casual attitude about it was even more reassuring than her words.

'I really need a massage,' she said. 'This Sunday would be great.'

Perhaps there was a lesson here, a lesson I had learned before. I myself always, always said something if a man got an erection while I was giving him a massage. Because I know an erection can be embarrassing to a man. We often get erections from physical stimuli that has nothing to do with any overtly sexual frame of mind. Pitching a tent doesn't always happen on purpose. Of course getting an erection, the male body is wired to initiate the process that eventually, hopefully, ends in orgasm. So I let my clients know I've noticed the erection, that they shouldn't be embarrassed because I know it's nothing personal. Saying something allows me to make several important statements. The essential message is:

'I see it; it's OK, and I expect you to let it go.'

Appropriate deflections when erections happen - at the very moment they happen - are important. Women know a lot about how to cause erections, if not by extensive field study, then simply by having adequate powers of observation. But not having the same equipment, they can never know for sure how it feels to have such an independant appendage. A woman might become stimulated by having a very sensual day, or by seeing a man who appeals to them on the street. But the arrousal doesn't push against her jeans, and it may not show.

Even experienced massage therapists can be confused about what such a blood rush might mean in any given situation. Once, when I was getting a massage trade at the club from Christine, she asked my opinion about an episode that had happened to her several nights before. She explained that she had begun to do outcalls at the home of a club member on request.

'I was at this guy's house and finishing the massage', she said. 'I generally tell people to take their time getting up from the table. But before I could say anything, he jumped off the table naked, and asked if he could borrow my oil. I handed it to him and he walked into the bathroom, leaving the door open behind him. I was folding the table when I glanced toward the bathroom door, and saw him oiling his penis. He didn't have an erection, but I was shocked. A few minutes later he came out in a robe, paid as if everything was completely normal, and said goodbye.'

'It doesn't sound normal to me. If I was you, I wouldn't go to his house again.'

40

'Believe me, I won't. What bothers me is that he has now made an appointment to see me here at the club. And I don't know what to do about it.'

'And you've seen him before?'

'This didn't happen until the third time I went to his house.'

'Did he ever do anything else which you considered odd?'

'Once - when I had folded the sheet down to expose his abdomen - he inched it down further.'

'With you watching?'

'When I turned to get the oil.'

'How far down did he move it?'

'To his pubic hair. When I noticed it, I turned to get a towel to cover him. When I turned back with the towel, he had inched the sheet down some more. I put the towel over him to the original place I had put the sheet.'

'And ...?'

'That was it. Nothing more happened, and I forgot about it.'

'Maybe you could call him before the appointment. Explain why you've become uncomfortable. Ask him to reschedule with someone else.'

'I don't even want to talk to him.'

'I wonder if we have the right to refuse service to members? We certainly ought to reserve that right. Maybe you should talk to management about it. Maybe all we have to do is put up a sign.'

Christine elected to talk to the manager of the club. To her amazement, the manager arranged a lunch meeting with the oily member. We thought this was rather amazing. Did the manager plan to tell this man there was no charge-code for penis oiling? Don Johnny threw a fit. Was outraged and threatened to sue for defamation of character.

The situation continued like a long, slow shudder.

Our supervisor informed us that we would have to continue to offer Don Johnny massage because they were afraid of legal action. And legally after all, Don Johnny had oiled his own member in his own bathroom. A tight rebuttal could hardly be made about the lowering of the sheet.

Don Johnny made an appointment with another masseuse. Of course, we all knew the story by that time. Don Johnny asked the second masseuse if she was willing to do house calls. She declined, saying she never did house calls. It quite naturally made her nervous being alone with the suddenly nortorious Don Johnny.

Several weeks later, Don Johnny made an appointment with me. I had plenty of time to think it over, and I made up my mind I would treat him like anybody else, and give him the best massage I could. I reasoned that being a man might render me immune to his urge to pull the sheet down. As if having a penis of my own might be similar to having a polio vaccination.

When I came into the room, he was on the table and covered with the sheet. I noticed he was still wearing his watch.

'Would you mind removing your watch? We may as well transcend time, since we both know you're here for a long, slow hour.'

Taking off his watch, he said:

'Here; put it in my right pants pocket.'

His pants were hanging from a hook on the wall. His underwear was protruding from his right pants pocket. Which meant I would have to touch his underwear in order to put the watch in the 'right' pants pocket.

Tending bar, you soon notice that troublemakers immediately tip their hands. Some little quirk, surrounded by an air of oddness, telegraphs the unhappy situation. If he hadn't specified which particular pocket to put the watch in, I wouldn't have experienced the dance of neurons that alerted me as I stood looking at his protruding BVD's.

I put the watch in his left pants pocket.

There was nothing I could say to him. He hadn't done anything I could make an objection about without seeming extremely petty. I reminded myself that I had determined to treat him like anybody else.

After the massage he was extremely appreciative. He complimented me on my 'professionalism'. When I heard his choice of compliment, intuition told me he had gathered that I was aware of the circumstances surrounding his questionable status as a massage client. I experienced some relief that he knew that I knew.

He became a regular, weekly client on my books. He was normal and reasonable except for minor details, which hardly compelled me to form a damning judgement.

Sometimes he wouldn't close the massage room door when I left the room so he could undress in private. Maybe he hoped I was a peeper, but I never looked, so I don't know whether he was oiling his member or picking his teeth. Anyway, a cracked door was hardly a federal offence.

Several times, instead of undressing, he made a telephone call. But it was his time, he could waste it as he would. I waited 'till he got off the 'phone and gave him time to undress, entering the room when I heard the squeek of the massage table.

After each massage he was full of compliments. All that butter made me a trifle nervous. He said I was 'the best', adding that he had gotten massage all over the world.

One of my colleagues at the club had a business card that said 'The Best'. Which amused me when I saw it. Where massage is the subject, nobody is 'the best', because massage isn't a quick draw contest. One person resonates to another person's energy and touch for many reasons. Many of them are unconscious and will always remain that way. Technique is the least of it, although skill levels of touch do vary widely.

Possibly Don Johnny had thought out his situation relative to the massage staff and club management, and concluded that getting his massage from a man was the best way to avoid naughty inclinations. I was perhaps, his righteous white wash. A haven from the nasty storm of rumor being whispered about him. And having made the decision, he was able to relax. So for him, I was 'the best'.

Well, perhaps.

There was some bad boy stuff, but it wasn't sexual. He made several appointments he didn't keep. The second time it happened, I told him I had charged him in his absence as it was club policy. The third time it happened, I felt I had to do something other than simply charge him again for a massage he hadn't had. Because essentially, I'm a wet sponge. A water person. And water people are wet sponge people. We have a hard time being tough.

When he came again, I told him again about the charge policy before giving him a massage. But soft- peddled it, by saying this one time, I would only charge him for half an hour, though I would give him an hour. He tipped me well to show his appreciation.

A week later, his secretary called me twenty minutes past his scheduled appointment, to say he was stuck in traffic and wouldn't be able to make it. All in all, he was a good and steady client, so I didn't charge him, but wondered whether I was making a mistake.

The following week, he again tipped me handsomely, but it wasn't enough to cover the amount I had lost by not being able to schedule someone else for the appointment he had missed. I made up my mind I would charge him full price if it ever happened again, no matter how often it happened. I didn't want to lose money on him, and I didn't want to ratify his inclination to cancel appointments at the eleventh hour.

Was this a challenge of some sort? Was I seeing the return of Don Johnny, the man who appeared to forever push the limits of acceptable behavior?

Massage may titillate people experiencing a very sexual phase of being; may beg churlish behavior in people carrying unreleased anger; or bring out a tendency for sexual perversion in people who have a tendency to be perverse.

I saw Don Johnny twice after that. He mentioned that he hadn't been to see me because he had bought a 'shiatsu' table, a table with an electric motor. It had rollers that traveled back and forth beneath the table. There were three speeds. I couldn't avoid thinking about him lying on his electric table, free at last to do as he pleased

44

while getting a 'massage'.

When he first came for massage, he mentioned he had recently been divorced. The last time I saw him, he told me he had just been married. He was fifty five years old. I knew that, because we had every client fill out intake forms before they got their first massage. He once mentioned he had two sons from his previous marriage. It seemed a good thing he had no daughters. Most likely, he was a man railing against loneliness and the loss of his family during the period when we worked with him; trapped with his own sexuality, and no outlet.

Lots of people come to massage in times of difficult transition. The person on the table is often an agitated edition of himself, on his way to a future unknown.

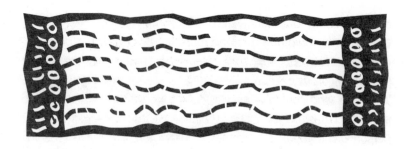

IN A PLACE OF SILENCE

Not everyone in the health club was unhealthy. The percentage of oddballs was probably on a par with the society that surrounded it. In the club however, society was magnified. And in the massage room, it seemed like the magnification was increased by a factor of ten. The club was a kind of North American social science lab, the creatures wearing lycra and spandex, rather than amoebic skins.

There were mirrors everywhere, it was all about the looking glass, and all very upscale. There were high-impact and low-impact aerobic classes morning and night. One instructor was nicknamed Sergeant Major Mary, because she screamed into a microphone like a drill instructor, reminding me unpleasantly of my Marine Corps days. The weight lifters and body builders had more social contact with the mirrors than they did with other members. The racquet ball players stuck together, the handball players compared their pains. The basketball players complained about the aerobics people not letting them finish their games. The aerobics instructors complained about the basketball players. Management tried to be pals with everybody but the staff.

Single people joined, hoping the club would be an opportunity to meet that special someone. Aspiring business people joined hoping to make valuable business contacts. Exercise junkies came twice a day to as a way to push away the world. A few walked the locker rooms looking like death camp survivors, but feeling way too fat, because eating disorders weren't uncommon. Some people were too fat, and would have profited more by a visit to a spa that specialized in fat reduction, than they did by trying to make the fat perform vigorous exercises.

People who couldn't imagine what touching other people as a profession must be like, often asked how we could stand giving a fat person a massage. I do confess it was more enjoyable touching someone with good muscle definition, because it was easier to trace the muscles when fat wasn't an obstacle. With fat people, there were basically two types. There were those who were packed into their skins like sausages about to burst. And there were those who had fat that rolled back and forth on their bones like jello. With the sausages, a lot of pressure and elbow work was necessary. With the jello, the best you could do was gently rock the person with the kinetic releasing rotations, which are very relaxing and beneficial. People who asked the question about what it was like to touch fat people, didn't know that compassion is the prime motivator for massage therapists, not a desire to touch beautiful bodies. It was the soul we were trying to touch, not the body.

The physical variables were interesting, of course, and endless. Until you've touched one hundred people in a very complete way, you may never realize how various we all are. We may have the same parts, but even in the same body, distinct changes are always happening. A calm, relaxed body barely resembles the same body undergoing anxiety and trauma.

People tend to get massage when they're experiencing trauma. They sometimes arrive looking like paper cut-out patterns; with inked dash marks delineating exactly where the radiologist is aiming the x-rays in order to kill the cancer cells. Some are handicapped by malformed or amputated limbs. They come after a death in the family, when they've been fired, lost a lover or been laid-off, when the divorce is finally final, when they discover they're terminally ill, or after a surgery. They come with organ replacements. They come in diapers. They're young and old. Some are beautiful, in great

47

shape, and mentally impaired. Some are ugly, with personality and great inner beauty. We felt honored to have work which allowed us to bring anyone, whether they were incredible physical specimens, fat or famished or sore, an hour of peace.

Aside from all the benefits mentioned by the marketing department, the whole thing was quite a peep show; and an expensive peep show. Nobody who wasn't doing better than average in his or her chosen field of business could afford a membership.

Which also made the club an ideal place to escape from the poor.

The gatekeepers were the front desk staff. They wore the club logo prominently displayed on identical shirts. The police were often called, to shoe away spare-change artists, who tended to set up 'shop' at the front door. Unless you were the guest of a member, or had a membership card, you were refused entry.

As staff members, our membership was a given, from the day we were hired. Most of us couldn't have afforded a membership or the monthly dues, if we had been required to pay for them. We were rubbing shoulders with doctors, lawyers, celebrities, visiting film stars, local on-camera news people and professionals of every kind.

The gatekeepers had a horrendous job during peak hours, when a crush of members came streaming through the door, impatient to trade their membership cards for a locker key and a towel. The turnover at the front desk staff was extremely high, which meant scheduling mix-ups for the massage staff, since massage appointments were taken at the front desk. The front desk staff was poorly paid, and they were expected to remember everything. It was a complex job. When it was busy, so much was forgotten. Especially when there were fifty impatient people demanding service. These difficulties resulted in many communications breakdowns. Appointment mix-ups were common, and appointment problems were very costly to the massage therapists.

Management decided the only way to improve these problems,

was to put a telephone in the massage room. Having a ringing telephone in a massage room is a dubious idea, but it did fix a few problems.

I heard some interesting, one-sided 'conversations'. For instance:

'Hi booby ...

'We could tat up the toolbox ...

'So you have a green beard?

'The Ferrari?

'Bali by April ...

'The Lamborghini, always the Lamborghini ...

'Filberts ...

'Actually, I'm getting a massage ...

'He's working on my calf ...

'OK. By sweet.'

'Interesting conversation,' I said. 'Did you feel like James Bond?'

'What?'

'Like Double O Seven. In the movies. Talking on the telephone while some guy in a white T-shirt pounds on your legs.'

She laughed.

'It might help if you were wearing a white T-shirt. Actually, I felt more like the Material Girl.

'I can't make heads or tails out of what that conversation could possibly have been about. The expensive cars for instance, the green beard. And how do you tat up a toolbox?'

'My husband is on a diet. He's lost forty pounds. When he asked me what we could eat for dinner, I said we could tat up the toolbox. We have a jacuzzi at the house. My husband has a white beard. When he stays in the jacuzzi too long, his beard turns green. He's a dealer of luxury cars. And he's just made a deal with a man in Oregon who wants to buy the Ferrari he's renovated. We've been talking about a trip to Bali for years, but my husband won't go until he sells the Lamborghini he bought in September ...

'And Filberts,' she finished, 'is what I always say when the expletives have been deleted.'

Working at the club was an unusual association with the elite and the lucky. An experience in learning to associate with people of every craze and kind.

There were a number of thieves among the captains of commerce. Towels were stolen to the tune of several hundred a month. There seemed to be an attitude that the towels ought to be taken home, since membership dues were so astronomical. Someone on the massage staff suggested that management buy pink towels, but management declined on the pink towels.

The towels were draped around necks and tied around waists, and sometimes worn as makeshift robes on women coming into the massage room. The massage room existed between the men's and women's locker rooms. And people arrived for their massage fully dressed and fully naked. It was quite astonishing when the door opened, to see an entirely naked woman walk into the room. The unexpected jolt that ran through my body was something like a mild electric shock. But I didn't mind; it was OK, I could take it.

As a man, I was thrilled to have a job where naked women, complete strangers to me, sometimes appeared. As a professional, I experienced some confusion about it. I could certainly appreciate that the skin was the largest organ of the body, but I was never completely prepared to see the whole organ. As a male animal, I was sometimes aroused. It did seem like there were women who were without embarrassment about being naked, and simply didn't give it a thought. Sometimes, it was clear they were exhibitionists, glad to have an opportunity to show themselves to a fully dressed man.

Our brochure explained that the normal procedure was to allow the massage therapist to leave the room while you undressed and got under the sheet. That you were free to wear whatever made you comfortable; that you would be draped at all times so modesty could be assured. Some removed everything, including diamond engagement rings and wedding bands. Nowhere did the brochure say to just strip down and strut your stuff. Yet, there were strutters, both male and female. And many of course, didn't read the brochure. Some had never had a massage before, but were bold. I would leave the room but when I returned they would be lying naked on top of the two sheets, rather than between the sheets.

It was amazing how different everyone was. How people acted, what they wore or didn't wear, helped to define the massage I gave. If people wore their underwear, the massage was more conservative. If they were completely naked under the sheet, the massage was more liberal. I might feel free to work on buttocks muscles or not for instance, depending on attitude and underwear.

It was sad, sweet and revealing to see how modest and perhaps scared, some people were. They might continually check the sheet, to make sure they were covered. They might not take off any jewelry and simply lie face down with their hands in fists nestled in on their chin, shoulders in the protected turtle position, as if preparing for a bomb raid. Some would lie down on the table fully dressed and look at you as if trying to determine whether or not you had a weapon. Most of the time, it only took a few reassuring words and a couple of minutes of touch to change the attitude, whatever it might have been initially.

I realized early on that the act of lying down and allowing someone to touch us, often induces a trance state. Because the tendency during massage is to follow each sensation as it arises in the body. A kind of interior scanning is the result, and interior scanning is a technique common to trance induction. One tends to follow the hands of the practitioner as they move from place to place. Getting the subject to follow any particular technique, is part of what is called in hypnosis 'a yes set'. The subject is given many verbal suggestions that can only be answered by a yes. And after many yes answers are given, the hypnotic suggestion is included in the yes set. The strong tendency is to accept the suggestion. With massage, the person getting the massage may not be saying yes to any particular statement, but being touched feels so good, they might as well be saying yes to each stroke. Which makes them inclined to accept suggestions.

I had a psychotherapist in California who used hypnotic storytelling and I had found it so fascinating that I had been doing an independent study for years, concentrating on the master of trance tales, Milton Erickson. I began to use Erickson's 'teaching tales' in the massage setting. I was a natural storyteller anyway. I wasn't like an encyclopedia salesman knocking on every door, and no doors were slammed in my face as I began to ad-lib the stories.

Eventually, when the structure of Erickson's intent became as clear as mineral water, I began to tell stories of my own. Based on Erickson's structure, but concerning events in my life. Sometimes I would go into a guided imagery induction, and eventually discover that I was the only one in the landscape I had created. I was on the beach, staring at the pebbles or admiring the lofty mountains. My client was still at the club, lying on the table, wondering what in hell I was doing on the beach.

My only goal was to assist people in relaxing more deeply, and being boring is a pretty good trance induction too, so I was usually effective. I had always been good with words and until one particular client, I'm sure I often talked too much.

One day I thought I heard a client say - when I asked her what she did for work - that she was an Ideologist.

The very idea of being an Ideologist just intrigued me right out of the room. I imagined being in Cuba consulting with Fidel Castro on Ideology. Maybe there were some tricky philosophical somersaults he needed to bounce off the Kremlin. Which is why he had consulted me, a professional Ideologist. Possibly newspaper editors called in Ideologists from time to time, though I had worked on the San Francisco Examiner as an editorial assistant, and I had never heard of one.

'What does an Ideologist do?' I asked her.

'What?' she said.

'An Ideologist, what do Ideologists do?'

'Can you talk into my left ear. I don't hear well out of my right ear.'

'Oh,' I said, walking around her head. "I'm just so curious about Ideology.'

I was talking very loudly now so she would be sure to hear me.

'What about it?'

'I mean, what does it entail?'

'How should I know?'

'I thought you said you were an Ideologist.'

'No, Audiologist. You know, hearing tests. Industrial noise recommendations, hearing aids.'

I was amused I hadn't heard her correctly. My whole internal conversation was the product of a hearing problem. I decided to shut up.

And began working on her head. When my hands came close to her ears, there was a high squeal, and I withdrew my hands.

'What was that?' I asked.

'A feedback squeal from my hearing aids.'

'Look, why don't you take them off? We don't need to talk. It will make the massage better.'

She took off the hearing aids and I put them on the table.

In massage school we often practiced massage with a blindfold on. Not being able to see increased the reliance on touch as a way to access a different sort of vision. Not seeing, we rely more on the sensations picked up by the hands, the ears and the psyche.

Working with her, realizing she couldn't hear, I began to think about how it might be to live in a silent world. The Public Address system could be heard in a muffled way, in the massage room. She didn't hear it. Voices from the men's and the women's locker rooms were audible, but she didn't hear them. The wall clock was ticking, but she only heard silence. The telephone in the massage room rang. She didn't react, and I let it ring.

I noticed that my hands had grown larger; that my tactile sensations were increasing. And gradually, I developed a negative hallucination for the sounds that surrounded us both. It happens all the time to people that live, as I once had, under an airport. The mind simply blocks out sounds that disturb the body, or the sounds that have such a monotonous quality that there's no point in hearing them. I was sinking into a sympathetic deafness, and soon was with her in her silent world.

In that world everything was, in a strange way, louder. Thoughts were amplified, arcs of bio-electric buzzing couldn't be heard but they could now be so clearly felt that they tickled the fingertips. Hot and cold areas of her body were as distinct as night and day. I was experiencing a tiny example of what it might be like to be deaf, and having the experience made the way I had been before seem dumb. My sensations were screaming at me, as if I had a hearing problem.

Every week she came back. Because for her as well as for me, something was being discovered. She was the advanced master of knowing what I was learning each time I saw her. And I gave her a place where she could be with someone without trying to read lips or straining to hear what was said.

Every time I was with her, my skills increased. My ability to be silent grew. My ear was to the wall of my own belly, so I began to hear my intuition more clearly. The time I spent with her passed quickly, yet slowly, fully. My hands had become more curious hands. They were listening with larger ears. They were radar hands, catching incoming blips.

Simple phrases, absolutely naive phrases, carried big messages to the mind.

'That's what it feels like here.'

'It's like this, when I touch like that.'

'This muscle is so very, very long.'

'Ankles are really fancy items.'

'What a soft place this is.'

Such phrases were full of portent, though they seem so banal. It wasn't what the words meant as much as where they meant I was.

In a simple, uncluttered place, reduced by silence to a childlike simplicity. I had crossed beyond the wall of knowing, and entered an attitude of prayer.

MONTE CRISCO

THE COUNT

"ACCEPT ANY SUBSTITUTE"

INVISIBLE SHOES

Touch might be called the Mother Tongue of all language, and in the realm of touch, the woman is King. Both sexes are taught touch by mothers, and touch is quite a teaching tool. It's the only pre-language teaching tool, and it's anything but basic. Touch teaches intelligence through the hands of even the most unschooled mother, and expressions of affection and anger are the least of it. The real lessons of touch may have to do with coming into a physical existance in a world which produces, pain, awe and obvious magic. In this world nothing is nailed down, nothing is known and nothing exists but nuance. The translator for this realm is nearly always a woman's touch.

Women have the big engines in the emotional world of touch. In the world of massage therapy, they also rule. They rule by numbers (there aren't many men working in massage), they rule by inheritance (it's OK for a woman to touch almost anybody, but men are suspect), and (consequently) they rule by success. Men are often still managers or creative founders, but women pull the strings. If not through sheer numbers, then because without them, there would be very little business.

Though I was once the director of a massage program, I wasn't much of a manager. My nature is passive and contemplative. The whole idea of 'management' is alien to me. For me, it comes a little too close to judgement. As far as management goes, one of my prime regrets in life, is not being able to manage to give myself a massage. This isn't as narcissistic as it sounds, although modestly I must say, I'm really quite good. I could administer self-massage of course, and I did on the odd sprained ankle, or to give myself foot reflexology as a shotgun approach to any particular problem I might be having. But what would a massage given by me feel like? I could never really know.

In time I would trade massage for dental work, for legal advice, for Oriental imports, for rent, even for meals in an upscale French restaurant. But the best trade of all, was trading for touch.

Although I couldn't know what getting a massage from me feels like, I could know what getting a massage from my colleagues, was like, and I knew it as often as I could arrange it. We traded massages at the club at least once a month, on average. Which often meant several massages a month.

In the salon where I had worked for a time, I had traded massage for styling, for manicures, for pedicures, even to have permanent waves curled into my hair. And although all of these luxuries may seem frivolous to those who have never experienced them, they decidedly don't seem that way when you do experience them. How they seem, is wonderful, and natural. When you consider that in nature, 'grooming' and preening are completely necessary, it doesn't seem a stretch to contemplate the thought that, as human beings, we might do well to consider allowing ourselves some of the most common experiences that animals have every day in the wild.

Getting lots of massage, I began to know the value of getting lots of massage. It had nothing much to do with self-indulgence. It did have a lot to do with self-esteem, and with the need, one might say the illusion, of being cherished. Because when we're touched, we feel cherished and valuable. Is being touched and feeling valuable because of it, an illusion? And does it make any difference, if it is an illusion, as long as it makes us feel valuable? We need touch, and seldom know how much we need it, until we get it. And years can be lived, or half-lived, without having any touch.

Which is a shame.

Touch makes us feel good. The body responds to being touched with a happy zip-zapping of neurons. And the brain in response, experiences a cacophony of joy. Is this electrical stimulation forgotten by the body as soon as the touch ceases? No. The after-effects continue. There's a decided aftermath. Many speak of a change going on for days. Is touch something craved by the mind? Definitely. Can you be a massage junkie? Sure.

There was a member of the club where I worked who craved touch. Maybe he was completely lonely in life, and touch was something he just couldn't find, unless he paid for it, since he appeared to be a complete creep. I realize I've automatically turned in my awareness badge by succumbing to name calling, but this man would give the word rectum a bad name. The man wasn't just a rectum, he was an extremely tight italic rectum; a bold rectum; a rectum with a drop shadow.

But forgive me, I'm being harsh. A rectum is to be admired, really. It's a complex sphincter muscle, isn't it? How amazing that such a muscle can retain fluids and yet open at the appropriate time to release what the body no longer needs.

This client wasn't really a rectum then, since he retained, but did not seem to know how to release. Jerk is probably more accurate. A jerk with money too, since massage isn't exactly cheap. Of course, when you play it against some of the more expensive habits, like tobacco and alcohol, it isn't really that expensive, either. Still, the jerk was spending more on massage than I was spending on lodging.

What brutal experiences had brought the Jerk to jerkdom?

How could I, not being his mother (or even a woman) teach him through touch? How could I translate nuance for him? How could I convey (in the best management style of my times) the imagination it would take to show him that kindness was its own reward? How could I bring him, through touch, an understanding of the benefits of an altruistic heart?

The answer was, I couldn't do any of those things.

Among the massage staff we called him The Count, which was

short for the Count of Monte Crisco. We called him The Count because he was quite hairy, and it took a lot of oil to give him a massage. Crisco was the brand name of a cooking oil, which is where the name came from. It wasn't an accurate name, since none of us would have considered using Crisco vegetable oil for massage, but accuracy has never been a real important part of name calling.

What we did use for oil was almond oil, or sesame oil, or coconut oil, or olive oil. The only oil that wasn't ever used, was mineral oil, since it clogged the pores. People bought pre-mixed massage oils; mixtures of peanut oil, almond oil, sesame oil and lanolin, if you could believe the labels. But the pre-mixed oils were dreadfully expensive and soon, many would settle on a preferred oil or lotion, one that didn't throw too big a dent into the pocketbook. Although the thought might not be engaging, the truth was, butter, or margarine would work in an absolute pinch.

When you gave The Count a massage, you had to pour on the oil. 10/30 wasn't thick enough. 10/40 was more like it. You just had to pour it on. Until his hair was nearly waving in it like seaweed on a beach. Otherwise, there was no glide and you were simply pulling his hair with every stroke. Which he naturally wouldn't have liked.

There were many things that The Count didn't like. And he wasn't shy about telling you what they were. Or about telling you what not to do. When he came into the room, it was as a privileged person. He entered as though he was disappointed, somehow. Entered with derision, anger and impatience. As though he was annoyed to find you there, rather than the harem he deserved.

His attitude had nothing to do with sex however; it had more to do with privilege and a kind of paid bondage. He had bought time, and the lowly rubbers (of His Illustrious Body), be they male or female, were discounted. Everyone had the same experience with The Count. It was a bad experience. Which was exceptionally sad for many reasons, not the least of them being that (because he was such a meal ticket), you would have to see him all too often.

There isn't an established world-wide protocol in massage, but some clients really are annoying. The Count wouldn't remove his gold necklace, for instance, and it's very frustrating to be required to work around a necklace. He also disliked music, and would not allowed it played. Sometimes, when weary from having a full schedule on the books, music gives the energy to continue. The Count didn't like to have his face touched. He would often direct your attention to some particular place he might feel was an important place for you to spend more time than you had just spent. Which kind of made you feel like an attendant of some sort, perhaps a window washer. The Count was inclined to point at a spot on the window you had, in his opinion, missed. It seemed impossible to please him, no matter what. Many moaned and sighed with pleasure; The Count could only grunt. Any of these idiosyncrasies on their own, would have been fine. But taken altogether, they made him almost impossible.

One had to prepare carefully for an hour with The Count, or there was a very real danger of serious, post-Count depletion. There are energy vampires in the world, contrary to scientific opinion. Vampires who will drain you if you don't take precautions. The Count was such a beast.

He was, in addition to being quite dead, extremely dense. Some people are so dense, it's difficult to lift their arms. With heads so heavy, they remind you of bowling balls. The Count's head, was a wrecking ball with a face on it. It could not be lifted twice by anyone who wasn't (at the very least) one of the highest paid action heroes in Hollywood. If you lifted his head once, you put your arms under such a severe strain, that to lift it twice would be to risk torn tendons. The tip-off to the actual weight of The Count's head, and his torso as well, could be seen for as much as twenty minutes after he left the room.

The Count's weight impressed the table so forcefully that his outline remained, long after he retreated to his casket. The tissue memory of the three inch foam on the massage table was so gravely assaulted that the first time it happened, I feared the naugahyde amnesia would never lift. I thought I might be forced to buy a new table.

There should have been a crane in the room to pick up his legs. A come-along to roll him over. After you were finished with The Count, you were really finished, unless you considered wearing heavy-duty, protective space gear.

Hollywood pictures the healer as someone who momentarily takes on the illness of his subject, wincing or writhing as that pain passes through him. It isn't an entirely empty celluloid notion.

Touching someone is an actual merging on an energy level, and most massage therapists have experienced the pains of the clients they work with. This is possible, because touching someone, your bio-electric field merges with the person you're touching, whether you like it or not. Sometimes it isn't fun.

Energy transference happens so often - if you forget to take precautions - that the absolute necessity of having the right attitude when you touch someone is a completely pedestrian idea to anybody who does hands-on work. The principle precaution taken in giving a massage is called 'grounding'. The idea of grounding is taken from electrical terminology.

Contrary to the movie stereotype, someone who's working properly isn't taking on the other person's pain, but is working with what might be called an empathetic detachment. They aren't attached to results, and they aren't trying too hard. In fact they aren't trying at all. What they are doing, is allowing their field of energy to merge with the person they touch. The negative energy that enters is allowed passage through the body and into the earth. This is possible because a relaxed body, working efficiently, doesn't trap energy. If a healer is a resonant transformer (in electrical terms), without energy binding in his body (comparable to breaks in the circuit), then the energy is 'grounded'.

When I found The Count scheduled on my appointment books, I would first climb into the the imaginary, invisible, (but extremely *protective) 'Suck' Suit' designed in Norway by Brendon Boxbender, the famous Norwegian Suck Suit designer. The Suck Suit would greatly amplify the traversing of The Count's dead weight and joyless energy as it passed through my body. I would then put on and lace up the invisible 'Sender Shoes', which had jet nozzles on each of the heels. These nozzles could discharge black matter right into space at an amazing pace. The whole ensemble was augmented greatly by my Invisible Gloves. The gloves were intelligent gloves and perfectly balanced, since they had been in attendance at aggressiveness training seminars in California. This enabled them to refuse the admission of any particles of selfishness which The Count might try to impart, either willfully, or simply because he had so much to spare. With the invisible gloves on, my hands could remain upbeat and impervious.*

I could talk about the imaginary Golden Net, The Lines Of Connection, The Ball Of Light, The Brace Beams, The Spinal Tap and The Giant Earth Drill, but I would just be blowing smoke.

Actually, I never did put on the Sender Shoes, the Norwegian Suck Suit or the Invisible Gloves. But believe me, they are only a wee bit more fanciful than some of the grounding techniques taught as tools for centering in body work.

If my intention was ever to connect with The Count, I failed totally. I was grounded, I didn't float away, but I could hardly claim to be centered. Working with him was nearly always a trying experience. Maybe if I had been a woman, I might have found a way.

But I don't think so.

"FOUR MONTHS AGO, I HAD BREAST REDUCTION"

SIBERIAN MASSAGE CHART NOTES

SIGNALS FROM THE SENDER

My talking hands were sometimes telling tales behind my back. Because half the time I wasn't listening. I was reluctant to see myself in any way which didn't match my image of who I was. I was half-formed some of the time, ill-formed half the time, and blind to my shadow side. I had intuition and intelligence, but my insight was lacking. I was tapping out a tactile Morse code, and sending skin telegrams even when the telegraph operator was out to lunch.

I didn't always have people fill out intake forms but when I worked with a massage staff, we all shared clients who might come for a massage when one of us wasn't there. It was courteous to leave chart notes. The notes were brief: Surgery on such and such a date. Sore low back, wry neck, frozen shoulder, etc. Sometimes I didn't have time to make notes between clients, so I would complete the chart notes at night.

To club management, massage was a commodity, the more sold the better. The front desk booked people hour-to-hour, with no breaks between clients. We would say goodbye at about five minutes to the hour, and leave to wash our hands. If the client wasn't prompt about leaving, the next appointment might knock on the door when the next appointment hour arrived. It was all wrong. After a massage, you want to lie with it, luxuriate in it, bask in the glow, so to speak. But someone was knocking on the door. A client, male or female and wrapped in a towel, might open the door to the wrong locker room to see who was knocking. There wasn't any

63

partition between the massage room door and the locker rooms. Men and women in various states of nakedness could be outraged or nonplussed. Oddly, there were very few complaints about this casual state of affairs.

Although I would have preferred a fifteen minute break between clients, there was something exciting as well as exhausting about working without breaks. It facilitated an ability to make quick decisions. It encouraged an efficient approach. You had to ad-lib on your feet. This arrangement was even more compressed when there was a string of half-hour clients. Everyone on the massage staff had experienced working seven hours without a break. Sometimes that meant as many as twelve people had passed beneath your hands. There was a tendency to count clients when the day was done, calculate what the paycheck would be, and go home in an exhausted, satisfied state.

Given the situation, it was often impossible to make complete chart notes, or any chart notes at all. But chart notes and intake forms were important. If somebody had frequent headaches and my chart notes reminded me of that, I could spend more time on the head, neck and shoulders. If I saw even five people a day, it was hard to remember anything specific about anybody because people often didn't return for several months. It was embarrassing to me and insulting to the client, when I asked the same questions two or three times. Especially because massage is such a personal experience. People were apt to be disappointed when you didn't remember them. Chart notes were necessary but I considered them a nuisance. It seemed like a chore.

And my memory was very selective. I was born into a military family, which as far as moving is concerned, is the modern equivalent of being born into a gypsy clan. The uniforms were different, but home was where we were, not where we used to be. One of the lessons learned was to forget the past, concentrate on the present, and move into the future. Forgetting the past as soon as possible was necessary to survival, and beneficial to emotional well-being.

There was no conscious decision about it, it just happened. It was years before I realized I had cultivated a selective amnesia. Working in the massage setting brought it home to me.

Attentive salutations of hello and goodbye are always important, but especially important when they surround an extended touch. The posture and the tension we carry often feel 'normal' to us, and our tendency is to return to it after a massage. When we think we've had a transforming experience, we're more likely to 'fix' the change that has taken place. When the massage therapist abruptly ends the treatment and the goodby is casual, we're likely to lose the benefits we may have gained by 'falling' back into our 'normal' patterns by rising too quickly.

'That's my next client, so I have to stop now' is a meat cleaver sentence.

When I had performed what I considered to be a miracle of a massage, my tendency was to give the casual goodbye. Translated, the casual goodby seemed to imply that miraculous massage was my daily bread and butter, that as much as I'd like to stay, another miracle was waiting to be performed.

When I began to take insurance related massage clients sent by chiropractors and physicians, I began to make my chart notes more complete, though the massage was the same. It was necessary, because the insurance companies were paying the bill and they required medical terminology and precision.

But the chart notes I wrote at home gave me distance on the day. I began to throw in personal attitudes, chunks of family matter, particles of belly button lint. Sometimes I discovered something in the writing I hadn't noticed at the time of the touching. A reflection would produce a refraction, revealing a crack in the mirror I had failed to see.

Time was stretched by my more leisurely notes; something electrical began to buzz inside my head. The notes were setting me up for my next encounter with whoever I was writing about. The home notes became terse short stories. And writing them, I found that the past began to influence the future. An invisible harmony was created between the subject and the writer. My attentive evenings writing chart notes began to send out shoots, or ethereal roots, which wrapped me into my work on a new level. My attention seemed to gather my ability to be attentive. The skin telegrams became more intricate, involved, and silent.

Writing about others, a self-portrait began to emerge. I threw on the varnish, trying to produce a glossy replica of who I thought I was. It was quite stirring, but over time there was no way to avoid the fact that I was beginning to see a wooden Indian. A dimestore Dick Tracy wearing a massage table 'face-place' for a cravat. My headdress was a cornucopia of literary feathers, but they were chicken feathers, the feathers of crow, the tail feathers of mottled grey pigeons. Tracing scraps of conversation and memory with words, I began to hear echoes of myself in what I was writing; began to see that what I was writing, were signals from the sender.

My interactions with clients gave me more intimate contact with people than I had ever had. And when the people were women I found attractive, the situation was sometimes problematic. Sometimes I felt like a castrated harem attendant. At these times I was torn between loving my work and being a man. I would have been surprised to know that I was attractive to many women who were also clients, but even if I had known it, I would have been confused about how to approach them.

'Nice tissue, would you like to have dinner with me,' somehow didn't cut it.

I might have thought to ask if a client would consider having coffee with me sometime, but I still didn't think it was appropriate to entertain the idea of trying to make friends of clients. I was still trapped by my own professional demeanor. Because I was an ace at repression.

I was waiting in the massage room for an appointment one day when a woman came through the door covered in a towel. She was dark, petite and slender. She had a comic approach to life, and

66

startled me by her opening statement.

'Four months ago I had breast reduction surgery,' she said.

'Really? I've never known anyone who had that surgery.'

'My breasts were always a ball and chain anyway, so I finally decided to do something about it. I was hoping you could work on my scars.'

'Sure,' I replied. 'Go ahead and get ready. Just holler when you're all tucked in.'

I left the room so she could get on the table in privacy. In the men's locker room, I found myself leaning against a locker in a state of amazement. I was excited and astonished, but ready to respond to her request. A few things could be done to reduce scar tissue. Rubbing Vitamin E oil on scars facilitated the healing process. Scars could be broken down by cross-fiber frictrion. But breasts were made of fatty tissue, and cross-fiber friction was most effective where the scar existed in muscle tissue. Still, I would do my best. I had only been a breast doctor for three minutes, but I was eager to add to my clinical mastery of post-surgical breast manipulation.

One look at her made it easy to see why her presence, coupled with large breasts, could have caused her problems. She had a lovely dark face, with playful, sparkling eyes. Her hair was jet black, her body slender but curvaceous. The flirtatious style was also compelling. Apparantly she had the breast tissue removed hoping to solve the problem of being too attractive to men, but I could have told her already it wasn't going to work.

'I'm ready,' she said, her voice muffled by the closed door.

When I came into the room, I found her covered, the sheet up to her chin.

"Would you be willing to tell me about your surgery?' I asked, as I began to work on her face.

'I just decided enough was enough. The surgeon was a freind of mine and I requested a spinal anaesthesia so I would be awake and be able to see everything.'

67

'How remarkable,' I said. 'What was it like?'

'He sliced under the areolas,' she said, her voice softening, 'and rolled back the nipples so the unwanted breast tissue could be removed. He made an incision under the breasts near my ribs, and sliced away additional tissue there before returning the areolas and nipples to their natural position. Then he sewed them back to my body with a tiny, tiny needle. It took a long, long time.'

She was describing her breasts as if they weren't a part of her. 'The aerolas, the nipples, the breast tissue,' - and then - 'he sewed 'them' back to 'my' body. The breasts had been disowned. Probably hadn't been hers for years. They were a pair of nasty twins who had always caused her no end of grief.

It was understandable. There's a natural tendency to seperate ourselves from shoulders causing us trouble, 'bad' backs, 'stupid' feet, 'damned knees' and so forth. Mentally seperating body parts disconnects the healing process. The bad back is feared, loathed, hated because it causes us such pain. Accepting the 'bad' back, sending it acceptance and love, is the first step toward healing it.

Lying on her back on the massage table, she described the operation as though it was a pleasant dream she was having. Her voice was soft, slow and unemotional. I realized she had been given a sedative before the surgery and now, telling me about it, she had regressed into the stoned condition of her sedated state.

'Have you been pleased with the results of the surgery?'

'Oh yes. I'm not having back pain anymore and I'm sure it's because I don't have to carry around the twin peaks anymore.'

I explained that the first thing we had to do was realize she needed to give her breasts a chance to heal by sending them an attitude of love and forgiveness.

'They may have caused you trouble in the past,' I said, but they've been assaulted by the surgery. Every surgery, no matter how beneficial, is also experienced as a rape by the body. I'm sure you can feel compassion for your breasts if you think about it. Think of them as your children. They've been hurt. They need your loving kind-

68

ness.' By this time I had finished with her head, face, neck and shoulders.

'Let's have a look at these former tyrants,' I said, and slipped the sheet down over her breasts to her belly.

Whoever her surgeon was, I had to admire his work. He didn't leave her breasts in a state of exaggeration, nor were they diminutive. The stitches must have been very carefully taken, because they had nearly disappeared, leaving only the pink lines of her healing scar tissue visible. The only evidence remaining to provide me with a guess at the former size of her breasts, were the darkly pigmented areolas, which were a milk chocolate brown and approximately the size of two silver dollars. The thin rings around them were like faint memories of her incisions. They looked like pink halos around two caramel colored moons.

As I worked gently on the scars, her nipples distended.

'Your nipples are only distending because of increased blood flow,' I said, 'it's completely natural.'

But it wasn't completely natural. It was completely amazing. I was describing circles around a woman's breasts, her nipples were distending, and it was my job . When I got into hands-on work, I never imagined my hands would be quite so 'on'.

If she had been standing, the scars under her breasts along the rib cage would have been hidden. In order to work on them while she was lying on her back, I had to gently lift each breast toward her chin. Here I was, in my forty second year, lifting breasts for a living. I didn't know whether the distension of her nipples was connected to the sensual nature of the work I was doing, or whether the stimulation was awakening sexual desire in her, but I didn't dwell on it.

'I noticed, while working on your face, that you carry a lot of tension in your jaws.'

'My jaw was broken by my ex-husband.'

She said this passively, as one might tell a doctor some additional bit of health history. I didn't say anything. If she wanted to explain this memory, which seemed to fly into the room like a surprising

69

Raven, I knew she would.

Sometimes it was necessary to ask personal questions that might have a bearing on the injury or tension presenting itself. But asking about an unhappy memory, was risking the invitation of a trance regression to an unhappy time. Even if the person wasn't in a trance, they would be likely to bring the negative energy of the incident back into the body as they talked about it. Since I was a man, since her ex-husband was a man, there was the possibility of some confusing transference occuring.

When I went home that night, I wrote about what had happened, comparing getting a massage to going to a movie, where both events take place in a semi-dark room, exciting a sensual synesthesia that initiates a neural dance. That during the dance, unconscious memories and desires sometimes broke to the surface with the flash and brilliance of jumping fish. I wrote about feeling like a blind usher without a flashlight. I admitted that I too was sometimes subject to the dance - kindled as it was by fragrance, music, touch, and warmth - by the memories of other hands and other times.

The following week she came for another massage and I enjoyed seeing her even more than I had the first time. I was encouraged to think we could become friends. During the session, she was so vivacious and flirtateous, that I even began to think something more than a friendship might be possible. In the following days, I often saw her in the club, and she always gave me special attention. When I saw her walking through the club one day, she winked at me and out of her warmth and that wink, I was trying to build a rainbow.

When I had finished the writing, I thought it was an interesting piece. So I did something I had not done before while writing about clients under the auspices of chart notes. I gave it a title, calling it Anaesthesia.

She had mentioned that she had been a journalist before going into business in another profession. We had talked about writing; sharing observations about it, and laughing over how hard it was to

70

get it right. It occured to me she would be an ideal person to give me feedback, so I asked her if she would read it, and she said she would. I knew the piece indirectly conveyed my attraction to her, though not in any overt way. I left the sealed manuscript with her name on it at the front desk. It was returned a week later with no comment. And she began to ignore me when we passed each other in the club. I was totally surprised. After a few days I wrote her a note, apologizing if I had in any way offended her, and expressing the hope that we could be friends.

She never responded. It was a hard way to learn that women who have been sexually abused are sometimes very flirtatious and sometimes seem to invite a man toward the very behavior they may least desire. It's mentioned in many books about abuse and sadly, is one of the most common defence strategies in any legal defence. I've been extremely careful to camouflage anyone I've written about since.

And matured enough to be understandably suspicious of overtly flirtatious women. If a woman always swings her hips, it's metaphorically a hip problem, isn't it? If she's flirtatious with all men, it's obviously bogus. If she's only flirtatious with me, I'm naturally flattered and interested.

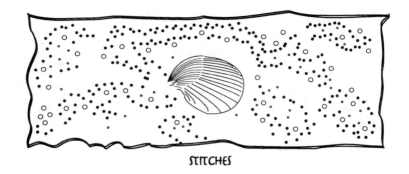

STITCHES

I moved into the Pike Place Market so I could be four blocks away from the club. There were always hundreds of tourists clustered at my front door adjacent to Pike Place Fish. It was a fertile environment. Exciting, noisy, and so dirty I had to clean the soot off my windowsills at least once a month. Street musicians played daily on the worn red bricks, and the best food in the state was at the bottom of the stairs.

On weekends in the early Spring I sometimes drove north to stay the weekend in my parent's beach cabin, which they only used in the Summer months. It was a ten minute walk from the parking lot, down a three hundred foot ramp, and along a boardwalk behind the houses. At the bottom of the ramp, a small colony of dwellings perched on bulkheads five feet above the water. Cabins on cedar log stilts aren't uncommon on the inland waterways of Puget Sound since the tidal drop-off isn't as sudden as it is on ocean front property. Sand bars tend to calm the local waters.

High tides at the beach wash in under the houses. When a high tide conjuncts with stormy weather, waves crash against the bulkheads and shoot into the air. The water is violently whipped across the decks, and after the storm, it's sometimes necessary to rake seaweed off the deck and throw it back to the beach.

When I heard that one of the oldest residents of the beach had just had a surgery, I went out to see him. I had chart notes to write, and the beach was a perfect place to do it.

72

Massage was becoming something like a tactile form of detective work. The 'leg work' was becoming less mysterious all the time, since backs and bellies couldn't lie the way lips easily could. My hands were taking notes during the day, and writing them down at night. My psyche and my self confidence were in a season of growth.

I had begun to have confidence about the skills I'd acquired. Begun to think I could have a healing effect on people just by being around them. I was rarely out of character. I was a character with a healing frame of reference. Some of the insecurities I once had about myself as a man, were now owned as advantages. My over sensitive nature was now a sword of sensitivity. With sensitivity, I was confident I could cut to the heart of the matter. I was overdoing it at times. Occasionally cutting to the heart of the wrong matter. Sometimes I even found myself giving touch unique to massage while making love.

I didn't think about it, but this new confidence was another kind of insecurity. I was becoming quite dependant on my new identity as a healer. It could have been worse. I could have become dependant on being an excellent cat burglar, for instance. I might have prided myself on stealing rings while kissing unsuspecting sweethearts. Or maybe I could have been a co-dependant plumber ...

Summer residents turned off their water at the end of the beach season to bleed the pipes, so they wouldn't freeze in the winter. A neighbor I hadn't seen in years was turning his water back on in preparation for the summer season. He asked me what I was doing these days for a living.

'I'm a massage therapist,' I said.

'Therapist, right,' he said, with grinning derision.

I didn't take it personally. When people heard you were a massage therapist, the reactions could range from interest to disgust. According to my license I was a massage 'practitioner', but massage 'therapist' was the vogue term. People in massage never called themselves practitioners. It sounds too much like we still

73

needed practice.

After opening the house and turning on the water, I took off my shoes and jumped down to the beach. Sand fleas bounded around my toes. A fat Robin was hopping along a log in search of a treat. Grey Guillemot sea pigeons were winging in to land in the water with their orange, duck-like feet. Seals were barking in the bay. Migrational sandpipers were feeding along the tideline. Winter tides had swept away the rocks and the sand was clean, damp and welcome to my feet.

Jim's house was only seven decks down the beach. His wife Zeldi was sitting on their porch. When she saw me, she began to lower the electric ramp Jim used as a boat launch, to the sand. I walked up the wooden incline to the deck.

'Hi Zeldi, how's Jim?'

'Hi Michael, good to see you. Why don't you go on in and see him?'

Jim was sitting in an armchair watching television. It was strange to see him sitting because even at eighty two, he was always an extremely active man. He seemed to be in a daze. He didn't see me until I spoke.

'Hi Jim, how you feeling?'

'I had a surgery Mike.'

'I heard about it. So how's it going?'

'Not too bad.'

He was lying. He looked like he had been zapped with a stun gun. He didn't even think about trying to get out of the chair.

'How long since your surgery?'

'About nine days.'

'Takes time to heal.'

'They sliced me up, Mike. I had six incisions to ream out my veins. Two in the wrists, two in the ankles, and two in the gut.'

Jim began to attempt to get out of the chair. He turned one way, then the other, like a rock climber trying out positions in an attempt to determine to best way to make his next move.

'Don't get up,' I said.

'Oh hell, it's time I moved. I've been sitting in this damn chair for two weeks.'

'You're moving pretty slow.'

'I'm sore all over. You wouldn't believe it.'

Bracing himself on the arms of the chair, he achieved a standing position, his face tight with the effort.

'Say Mike, you still rubbing bodies?'

Yes I was. I was the body rubber. Apparantly it was something like shining shoes or polishing apples.

'I'm still at it. How are the stitches holding up?'

'Look at this,' Jim said, and shot his sleeves.

He was holding his arms away from his body, his hands were two upturned fists. I looked down at the medial side of his wrists, which could have been the wrists of a recent suicide attempt, except they were both sliced vertically along the veins.

'Is this a Huckleberry Finn kind of thing, Jim? I've got a few scars of my own you know. Look at this!'

I pulled my sweat pants up over my knee to show him a scar I had from orthroscopic knee surgery.

'I don't see anything,' he said.

'That's because scars heal so well. Look, right here!' I said, pointing at the small remains of the inscision on the outside of my knee.

'And here!'

I pointed at the equally tiny scar on the other side of the patella. Jim wasn't impressed. I pulled up the other pants leg above my knee, and pointed to the similar scars I had on that knee.

'Two knee surgeries, Jim. And I've had two hernia surgeries, look!'

I pulled down my sweatpants and exposed a hernia scar not six months old. He looked it over.

'Pretty good,' he pronounced.

'The other one, on the other side has healed so well I can't find it anymore,' I said. 'But you're only two incisions ahead of me, partner.'

'But you're young, Mike.'

'The body doesn't care, Jim. It takes a little longer as you age, but the results are the same.'

I could see an idea sweep across his face.

'I'm going to show Mike the stitches,' he shouted to Zeldi, who was still on the deck.

He unbuckled his belt and released a snap button. His pants slid straight to the floor because he had lost a lot of weight. He carefully lowered his Paisley print boxer shorts to his knees. It was difficult for him to bend down. The sparse, recently shaved pubic hair wasn't half an inch long. There were two seven inch scars on both sides of his lower abdomen, which went an inch down his legs.

The flesh was still clamped together, each scar had six metal staples an eighth of an inch wide. The clamps were about an inch apart. Between the clamps, the flesh was pink, red, blue and grey. One bit of skin was rippled, like his skin was a shirt and the buttons didn't exactly match the button holes. The staples looked to be stainless steel, the size of notebook binders. Hard, efficient metal clamps, holding together the eighty two year-old flesh.

'Ever see anything like it? Jim asked.

My eyes were riveted to those scars and the stainless steel clamps piercing the inflamed tissue. The clamps were awful to look at, though there were probably many good reasons for using them. They were quick, easy and antiseptic. But my heart stopped to see them. Every warm emotion in me was repelled by those staples. On Jim's right leg there was a large green welt just beneath the scar. I reached out and placed my palm over it.

It was hot.

'What do you make of that? Jim asked.

'Your muscle has been shocked and outraged. They had to clamp the muscles out of the way so they could do the surgery. Bruised, that's all. It'll be OK. Takes time to heal, though. Have you got any vitamin E oil?'

'I don't know.'

76

'Well, if you've got vitamin E capsules, just cut them in half and use the oil to rub on you scars. The vitamin E will help you heal.'

Jim had become unsettled with the fact that he was standing there with his pants down. He gently leaned down and pulled them up. Then he sat back down and pulled up his pants legs, revealing the scars above his ankles.

'Feel my legs,' he said. 'Do you feel any circulation there?'

I put my palms around one of his legs, between the ankles and the calf. His leg was warm, almost hot. The pulse was good.

'Strong as a horse,' I said. 'Have you been out running?'

Jim looked doubtful. He looked discouraged. He was close to giving up. He wasn't sure he was going to make it. I wondered myself.

'I can't believe those stitches,' I said. 'If you weren't so ornery and tough, they could have used cat gut. They probably had to give up and borrowed a staple gun from a carpenter.'

I straightened up.

'How's the fishing, Jim?'

Jim was a notorious fisherman. He seemed to know where all the fish hung out. There were pictures of him on the wall standing beside Salmon almost as big as he was.

'They haven't been catching any,' Jim said. 'The fish are waiting for me.'

'Well, don't keep them waiting too long.'

For the first time that day a smile appeared on his drawn face.

After a while we said so long, and I went back to the house.

I was cold, so I wrapped myself in a green shawl my mother had knitted for me and sat on the deck watching the seagulls. It would never have occured to me that Jim would outlive Zeldi and still be alive ten years later.

His condition reminded me with sadness of my grandmother.

His stitches reminded me of a woman I had seen earlier in the week. She had come for her massage in a grumpy state. I asked her what was bothering her.

77

'I had some stitches taken and they're bothering me,' she said.

'Stitches taken for what?'

'I had a few more cysts removed.'

We had talked about her cysts before. She produced pea-sized sebaceous cysts all over her body on a pretty regular basis. They were benign fatty cysts. She was always having them removed. I had never thought about why. It seemed to me cysts were depositories the body created for material it couldn't use, but couldn't find a way to flush.

'You always seem to be having stitches taken. Who does them for you?'

'My plastic surgeon. Look at these stitches,' she said, pulling down the sheet and twisting around on the table to locate the latest removal site. Her breasts were now in full view. She was very proud of her nipples, which had dugs the size of stubby pencils. She almost always found a way to show them to me. I concentrated on looking at the place on her buttocks indicated by her finger.

'I don't see anything. Wait a minute, I'll get my glasses.'

I put on my glasses.

'Well yes, I do see something. Just a minute, now.'

I turned and got a magnifying glass I kept in a drawer.

Now I was looking through two lenses at her stitches. There they were. A minuscule fiber, barely visible with the naked eye, laced through the smooth tissue of her tush.

'Isn't that amazing work?' she asked.

'Amazing. How many surgeries do you think you've had now?'

'Well, I had liposuction. And I had my sweat glands removed. With the cysts I've lost track.'

'You had your sweat glands removed?'

'Uh, huh.'

I let it go. It was too absurd. It was like living in a steamy tropical climate on the equator and cutting the chord to the air conditioner. I suddenly thought I knew why she had become a cyst factory. She could no longer sweat. And sweating is one of the a major ways the

78

body rids itself of toxins.

She wanted to be perfect. She was perfectly in character with wanting to be perfect. She plucked her perfectly reasonable eyebrows, and painted what was left with a perfectly black pencil. She hid her face behind a make-up mask which I'm sure was awfully expensive. She dyed her hair. She was all American and like most Americans bought all kinds of junk to clog up her pores so they wouldn't emit an odor.

I had lived in London for five years, where people thought one bath a week was sufficient. I find body odors mysteriously appealing more often than I'm repelled by them. But I'm no stinker. I take a shower every day. If I work out and chop wood or something, I sometimes take three showers a day. I haven't bought underarm deodorant since I stopped wearing white socks with black slacks. It was about the same time I stopped wearing underwear that strangles me.

Let the body breathe!

I invited this lady out for a drink one night. And later, made the mistake of taking her back to my apartment, where I allowed myself to become extremely impressed with her nipples.

Until that night I was a massage therapist virgin. Chaste, pure and virtuous. Had never slept with a client and never thought I would. Having sex with someone who is first a client is probably a sure way to lose a client.

Sitting on the deck surrounded by my mother's shawl, a shawl created by each of the stitches she had taken with long needles to knit one, pearl one, knit one pearl one until she was done, I marveled at the variety of stitches in the world.

HURT METER

12   14   28
9   3   26   18   98   32
6   22   36

ON THE SOIL OF MOTHER MUD

If there was a massage therapy canon, sleeping with clients would be a no-no in the canon. Of course, massage therapists are people, and people often do end up sleeping with people they work with first. Human nature being what it is, there can be a tendency for sexual tension to develop in a setting as sensual as massage. Sensual stroking, no matter how professionally pure the intent, can bring sexual consequences because the line between sensual and sexual is an invisible one, and different from one person to the next. Any man on the street would guess as much, which is why most massage schools now include instruction in "boundary issues" and ethical conduct.

Consenting adults have always been consenting adults, but there's a huge difference between eventually dating someone who comes to you first as a client, and taking advantage of someone who has every right to expect professional conduct.

Any man might wish he could complain of being weary from too many sexual requests, or moan about how awfully irresistible he is, but nobody has trouble resisting legitimate massage practitioners because we try not to do anything that inspires resistance.

My only object is to facilitate relaxation. My only intent is to connect with people in a helpful way. I may tell stories that sometimes have a hypnotic effect, but I'm hardly a hypnotic storyteller. I may have a therapeutic effect sometimes, but I know I'm no psychotherapist.

I'd be surprised to find anyone anywhere, working as a legitimate *masseur or masseuse who didn't have the same altruistic intentions which are my basic motivation. Wanting to be helpful is almost a condition of doing the work.*

It's a case of the walking wounded wanting to help other bleeders on the soil of Mother Mud. If you haven't been there, you can't know the pain of being there. If you've been there, you want to help anybody currently there, because you understand the pain so well, because being there is very much the place you never want to be again.

You of all people, know how it hurts. But somehow you survived your own personal attack of the devils. Somehow you emerged from your own muddy bog. You were able to climb out of the depression. You made it out of the psychic pit. You know some of the toe holds and you want to share them out of empathy.

Maybe you were suicidal, but you didn't commit suicide.

Possibly it was only a matter of hanging on. Maybe you just waited for the true you to come home again and jump all over your self-pity so it would never get in your way again.

Maybe it was a failed marriage you somehow survived.

Maybe it was a love affair that brought up something so primal it scared you. Maybe you let it go, and discovered how letting go makes you stronger and allows you to grow.

Maybe you had been fired or let go, and found a better job because of it.

Maybe your mother was alcoholic, but you came to terms with it, forgave her, found the true person behind the booze and saved yourself in the process.

Not that you had wracked up more points on the Hurt Meter than anybody else, but you had been lucky enough to find work that gave you some way to use the past pain in your life.

There was a letter for me at the front desk, written on the stationary of the Public Prosecutor's office. It threatened legal action against the club on account of me.

At first I couldn't remember who the woman making the com-

plaint was. Looking through my chart notes, I began to remember her.

'Complains of arthritic problems,' I had noted, 'complains of arthritis 'all over my body.'

Now I remembered her. She had come in the previous week.

Arthritis is noted in all the esoteric manuals as a condition which affects the joints and comes accompanied by a 'stuck' state of mind. There are so many types of arthritis, it's stupid to make sweeping generalizations about it. But a little sweeping through the body/mind (psychosomatic) books of indications, did help to put my mind more at ease.

Arthritis scares people. Nobody wants The Arthur. Arthur is perceived as bone stalker who will never ever, go away. When Arthur is the named condition, it puts people in a helpless place. Doctors don't generally offer any special diet. And give you no hope that anything can be done about it. Chiropractors sometimes use the word arthritis as a splitting wedge, driving it into your brain to convince you that nothing but spinal manipulation can possibly offer any relief. Actually chiropractic manipulations can offer relief, because movement in the body is what liberates energy, and liberated energy feeds the system.

There's an excellent magazine, Arthritis Journal, definitely worth consulting. Japanese studies have shown that immersion below certain temperatures gives significant relief for arthritis. American Indian cures involve immersion twenty times in freezing mountain streams. Diet is a definite factor. An alertness to allergy inclinations is extremely important. Red wine and cheese, among other food groups, can cause arthritic reactions among some people.

How do I know? Where did I get my Ph.D.? I don't have one. But I do have The Arthur. And some of us become experts in our own condition when the condition becomes painful and doesn't go away. After we've seen the number of doctors we need to see to convince us seeing doctors has been no help, we go to the library. We go to the bookstore to buy the newest books. We consult a

Physician's Desk Reference. We recoil in horror at pages and pages of side effects caused by the miracle drugs of modern medicine. We ask relatives and other folks if they know any folk cures. If we've persistent and lucky, we find something that helps.

For me, having arthritic knees because of knee surgery, eating ginger often seems to help a lot.

When I read the letter (with a cc. to the manager of the club) threatening legal action, I was really, really scared I might get the sack. I had a bursting synovial sack state of mind the moment I read the letter. I needed cortisone shots through my eyeballs to calm my brain. And I was a person who would do everything possible to stay away from cortisone shots, having read about the side effects.

I knew I had done nothing on purpose to cause the woman pain, but she had felt pain, she blamed me, and now she was threatening suit. According to the letter, she had experienced pain during the massage, the pain had increased after the massage, and she blamed me for the pain she was having in her body! She had been to three doctors. They had not found soft tissue damage, but she knew the massage was the cause of her pain. In her mind I had caused her pain, she felt damaged (though three doctors could find no damage), and she would have reparation.

I was told by my supervisor that the manager of the club wanted to meet with me.

I had not skipped school, pulled anybody's ponytail, written any graffiti or sassed the teacher, but I was being brought up before the Dean! Called to the Principal's office! I feared expulsion. Nobody would ever want a massage from me again! I would be ruined and disgraced! Forced to write imaginary Chart Notes From The Dead Zone, like some Siberian outcast.

'Have you seen this letter?' the manager of the club said.

'Yes, I got a copy,' I said.

'Well, what happened?

'I have no idea. I've looked at my chart notes and the only thing she told me is that she had arthritis that hurt her all over her body.'

'She says she had to go to three doctors.'

'The doctors found no soft tissue damage. And I certainly did nothing to cause her any pain. She didn't say anything while I was working on her, so this has taken me completely by surprise. There could be some transference involved.'

'Transference?'

'Maybe she was mad at somebody, I put pressure on her so her muscles could release, and her anger got directed at me.'

'Do you think that's what happened?'

'I really don't know. My intent is always to help. In Japan they do talk about something called 'menken' which, roughly translated, means a healing crisis.'

'A healing crisis?'

'It just means sometimes you have to get worse before you get better. The body has to heal everything at the end of the day. The healer is merely the catalyst for change. The change may be for the worse, but the person has a quicker recovery because of the 'menken' brought on by the work.'

The manager got together with the club attorney. Weeks went by, and for me they were terrible weeks. I was waiting for the axe to fall. My neck was on the chopping block. Firing me would offer some satisfaction to the club member who thought I had hurt her.

Finally, after six weeks, a settlement was reached. The club paid the woman's medical expenses and gave her a free month of membership dues, plus $1,500 dollars.

Though I wasn't fired, I was forever more on a short leash at the club. Which really distressed me, since I knew I was completely innocent of any dark intentions. It was clear this woman must have felt justified in her demands, but just as clear to me, in fact as clear as mountain spring water, that her justification was without justification.

She was an attorney in the Public Prosecutor's Office, so prosecution was her inclination. Prosecution was her game. And I was her *gander. Some anger consumed her and she had come for a massage with a chip on her shoulder. I put pressure on the chip, so she would prosecute me publicly.*

Even though it was her chip.

After that experience, I joined the American Massage Therapy Association. Membership insures legal representation. The protection amount was a million dollars. Of course, the dues are necessarily high for that coverage. Not being an attorney, I couldn't sue anybody to come up with the cash. I dropped my membership after a year. I didn't have anything to lose, because I didn't have anything. My car was an old banger, I didn't own a house, and there wasn't enough money in my bank account to cover ten pairs of socks, much less a suit.

Several years later, a woman on the massage staff was also the subject of suit. She had to undergo a deposition. She fled to Hawaii, but the suit followed suit. Suit is awful. Do everything you can to stay away from suit. In her case, she had been charged with administering a chiropractic manipulation. After awhile, she probably wished it had been a successful strangulation. Over a year later there was a settlement.

The woman who brought the suit against this colleague came to me a year later for a massage. I was very careful not to press too hard. I gave her a kind of hands-off massage. A 'psychic' massage. An 'energy' treatment. Actually, an arid grazing. A dry cleaning, if you will. I was pretty afraid of suit.

A man in a bathing suit and a neckbrace would be my next 'victim'. When I saw him in the locker room, I started laughing. Neck braces are funny for some reason, I'm not sure why. But a neckbrace on a man wearing nothing but a bathing suit is hilarious. I knew him because he was the Director of the Aquatics Program. He was always in a bathing suit, because he was the primary swim coach at the club.

'You ought to let me work on that neck for you,' I said.

'I couldn't let anybody touch me now. You can't imagine the pain

I'm in. But maybe when I get better, I'll test you then.'

'You'll test me? Gosh, I hate tests. What happens if I flunk?'

'Twenty laps around the pool.'

'Twenty laps! You haven't seen me swim. It would take weeks. A chase team would have to come in to serve me meals.'

'Why don't you take swim lessons?'

'Why don't you let me work on your neck? When that neck gets better you won't need me. You'll throw me away like a pair of leaky goggles.'

'I'm telling you, I'm in severe pain.'

'What happened?'

'Nothing that I know of. It just started hurting a few days ago and it's getting worse every day. My doctor put me in the brace to restrict side to side movement.'

'What the hell,' I said, I'll let you test me. No charge. Or let's do it like this. You give me a swimming lesson every time I let you test me.'

'Maybe in a few weeks, after the meet is over.'

'The meet?'

'I'm in training for an important national meet.'

'That neckbrace is going to slow you down a bit.'

'Very funny. I'll be alright.'

'I bet you won't.'

'What makes you say that?'

He had competed and placed in the Olympic Trials the year before. He was fiercely competitive.

'I just don't think a guy who's afraid of a massage is going to win any national competition.

'You're a jerk, Winecoff. But I guess I've got nothing to lose.'

When we got to the massage room, he displayed a new definition for the word rigid. The man was a living piece of construction site rebar. He was the tin man. I was simply oiling the armor. He wouldn't breathe. Nothing I said about breathing could convince him to breathe. He wouldn't follow my direction. In his mind he was the coach, a leader of men. I was merely a rubber of bodies. The lowly body rubber, with all the prestige of a condom.

He was locked into a rigid struggle with himself. He wouldn't give up the struggle. The struggle was tied to the coming competition. If he gave up the struggle, he thought he would lose the coming competition by default. After fifteen minutes, I had to remind myself to breathe. After thirty minutes I knew he was still locked in a breathless competition with himself. Forty-five minutes into the massage he began to tighten up even more. Now he was a railroad tie. His determination holding him down like railroad spikes. By the end of the hour, I could tell he was hurting more than he was when he first came in the door.

He was upset, but he was in too much pain to bother with giving me a piece of his mind.

Two days later, he was feeling better. But he didn't connect his improvement to the massage. He again took the teacher role with me.

'Here's a learning experience for you,' he said. 'After you worked on my back, I felt worse. I'm sure you meant well, but I thought I ought to tell you.'

'Yes, you experienced a healing crisis. Sometimes you have to get worse before you get better. I pushed you over the hump.'

The explanation temporarily stunned him.

'How do you feel today?' I asked.

'The next day, I felt awful.'

'That would have been yesterday. But how do you feel today?'

'I do feel a whole lot better today.'

'The best thing you can do today is skip your workout.'

'No way. I've got to work out every day until the day before the meet.'

'You know what? You haven't been listening to your body. Your body has been telling you to take a break. If you take a break today, your body will reward you for it.'

Several weeks later, the day after the meet, he sought me out. I was astonished when he came running up to shake my hand.

'I broke three personal bests in the meet,' he said, 'And I feel like you were a part of it.'

I was really touched by his declaration. It doesn't feel good when you try to help someone, to have them think you've hurt them. He had tested me, flunked me, then been big enough to allow that we were on the same side all along.

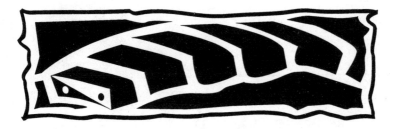

LINKS

I was cleaning out my closets when I found a small leather box I recognized as my father's. Looking into the leather-covered box, I realized it was a cufflinks/collar box. There was one white collar surrounding the circular, silk-covered centerpiece. The collar was starched, snow-white and pristine. Inside the center piece were some cufflinks, some without matching links to complete a pair. The cufflinks were good, working cufflinks, but who wears cufflinks anymore? The leather box was also useless to me, though it made me think of a time when stretching leather over wooden boxes wasn't so unusual.

I began to think about my father, a military officer for twenty seven years. Having been in the Marine Corps myself, I knew the meaning of 'leave'. Being on leave meant you had permission to exit or depart, to flee. But when my father was on 'leave', it meant I got to see him. For years I saw him every day, but even when he was home, he was too often away from home. Almost every afternoon he worked in the yard after coming home. Nearly every night there was some civic function he would attend. And when he was stationed overseas, a year could go by before he would appear.

Tucked in the corner of the leather box is a piece of paper with several lines on it in his distinctive hand; I recognize them as primer lines to a joke I once heard him tell about Kipling and Wordsworth in Timbuctu. It was a classy story, a gentleman's joke, only slightly ribald, very much like my father. His stories were never too much on the far side of crude. I never heard him tell the kind of story that makes your face feel like you ate something with too much salt on it.

Seeing these personal possessions made me recall the day my telephone rang and it was my mother, telling me my father was in the hospital.

'What's happened?'

'Nothing. But he's all yellow, like he has jaundice. You've got to go and see him.'

'Of course. Where is he?'

I made a note, canceled a few appointments, and went to see my father. He had turned an alarming shade of green. Several years later, when I went to a psychic out of curiosity, he asked me who had experienced jaundice in my family. I guess my father's jaundice scared me so bad I was still carrying the frightened aura of his illness.

To me my father was at first a God. And I had never got to know the God that my father at first was, as a flesh and blood person. He was always my protector. I knew, without any doubt, that if I was in trouble, he would be there for me. He might not be there to give me emotional support, but I had my mother for emotional support.

Seeing the God of my youth green made me slightly sick and afraid, even full-grown. It was assumed he had hepatitis. Exploratory surgery eventually revealed a pancreatic cancer. The tumor had pressed against the gall bladder, causing bile to flood his body cells. The surgery was only successful in bringing his color back to normal. Nothing could be done about the cancer.

While growing up, my brothers and I had observed on a daily basis, the starched salutes of Marine Corps guards as we accompanied our father though the main gates of whatever base we happened to be living on at the time. This show of military respect had contributed to the admiration and awe we had for our Dad. We loved and revered him with a subdued submission. We never made

90

a suggestion to him. He was a man who was always ahead of us. He had thought out all the angles before they occured to our young minds.

In the months following surgery, Dad began to lose weight. Within six months, he was reduced to lying in bed. Now he had time, nothing but time, to consider his life and his condition.

He began to make decisions which made it clear he was preparing for death. The first of these decisions was to direct that the garbage men come to the back of the house to pick up the garbage can which he had always taken out to the curb on Tuesday mornings. He had a new heating system with an automatic thermostat installed. It could be programmed to turn on the heat before you got out of bed in the morning, which he was no longer able to do. He had an alarm system installed so burglars wouldn't find it too easy to be burglars. He was thinking about a time when he would no longer be able to take care of my mother. He wanted to make sure she would have a safe, warm house when she got out of bed in the mornings.

He lost his appetite. He couldn't sleep well. His physician prescribed marijuana tablets to increase his appetite. The marijuana may have helped him to consider attitudes he might never have thought about before.

'Maybe you could give me a massage?' he said one day.

I gave him a long foot massage on the spot. He was very appreciative. I had forgotten that the big toe on his right foot (and half of his second toe) had been cut off by the lawn mower. I felt somewhat cut off myself, since I (who always had something to say) could think of nothing to say to him.

'Remember what Mom said when you came into the kitchen with a bloody sneaker?'

'Stay in the kitchen,' he said, 'I don't want you bleeding on my rugs!'

We both laughed, as it had become a family joke. Mom was completely compassionate but she had no idea how gravely my

91

father had hurt himself. All she saw was blood oozing out through the sneaker.

I made love to my father's feet. That foot massage included everything short of sucking his toes. After the massage, he asked if I would be willing to give him a massage every week.

On the way home I knew he was probably taking care of me the way he was taking care of Mom. I was living an hour away by car and coming to visit several times a week anyway. I suspected he had found a way to pay me for the two hour drive - coming and going - every time I saw him.

The highway stretched out before me, and so did my anticipation for the coming massages with my father. There had always been a physical awkwardness between us. It was a bittersweet lack of a touching tradition. Bitter because I had always wished he would reach out to me. Sweet because I knew it wasn't for lack of love that he didn't. Military men of his time simply weren't given to touching. Once when I came across a picture of my father holding me in his lap in my boyhood, the photographic evidence that he had once held me made me cry. Now I had a chance to touch him in a deeply symbolic way, if not in an actual embrace. Maybe he would discover how good it was to be touched by one of his sons. Maybe we would talk about things.

Sometimes I was so fond of the person I was about to massage I would look forward to the hour the way other people anticipate having dinner with a friend. Often I recognized a famous name, and my curiosity would be shot through with excitement. I had experienced eagerness about many massages. But I didn't always know how soon I would see someone again. I never knew I would see someone every week until they most probably died. And never before had the person in question been my father.

Previous conversations with my father were always lacking the casual familiarity that men share with one another. I was always his son and always aware of the way our blood bond cast a kind of anaemia over the things we were able to say to each other. Al-

92

though it has never occured to me until this moment, I think he was always trying to impress me by having all the answers. I was always so intimidated it never occured to me that he just wanted his sons to think he was great. Maybe now, all that would change. Maybe now we would talk like two people who no longer had time for posing.

When he suggested a weekly massage, I argued that I didn't want to be paid.

'I outrank you,' he said. 'We won't discuss it again unless you want a raise.'

He certainly outranked me. And I did need money. But what did rank have to do with it? In the car on the way home, I played the conversation over in my mind and added a few corrections:

'What does rank have to do with it? You may have been the Chief Of Staff of the Third Marine Division, but you're retired. You're a retired full Colonel with cancer! You're my Dad! I love you!'

In the first few weeks, Mom was in and out of the bedroom five times an hour. I pondered how to explain to her that the ideal setting for massage was a situation without interruption.

'Mom wants to be in here with us, Dad. I think she wants to get in bed with you. It's a pity I don't have four hands.'

'She hates to miss out on anything.'

'I know. But I wish she wouldn't keep popping in.'

I'm not sure what he said to her, but Mom left us alone in succeeding weeks.

I sometimes asked Dad to take off his watch. It seemed funny he would wear it in bed, but there was no clock in the bedroom and I suppose he wore it out of habit. His wrist probably felt naked without it.

'This is the first time I haven't seen you wearing your watch,' I said on one of my visits.

'I'm getting so thin it won't stay on my wrist. I asked your brother to take it to the jeweler to have a few links taken out of the watchband.'

93

Even in our solitude, the emotional confidences I had hoped for didn't occur. The answers to all the questions I had never asked, remained unasked and unanswered.

I had become skillful in drawing out my clients. Or maybe the confessions I almost always heard as a massage therapist, had nothing to do with skill, but were possible because I wasn't related to any of my clients. Maybe the confidences were a result of touching people who were at first strangers. My father kept everything to himself. Sharing his helplessnes and his fears wasn't his way. I was stuck with the silence he had always inspired in me. I was probably afraid that anything less than a 'manful' silence on my part, the kind of silence he kept himself, would be regarded by him as a weakness in me.

Where emotional truth was the subject, I was usually a blabbermouth. I often told interested strangers the most revealing confessions about myself. But being direct with someone I loved when something difficult needed expression, was something I had not yet learned. My father was extremely direct, but he wouldn't articulate personal emotions. His abilities weren't a part of my heritage. His direct way had driven me in an opposite direction. Our 'links' didn't match, even though we were on the same watchband.

One day my telephone rang.

'Are you coming to see your father this weekend?'

'Hi Mom, what's up?'

'A hospice nurse came today. She's a catholic nun, too.'

Mom's voice was lowered, slightly conspiratorial.

'That's really great. Of course I'm coming this weekend.'

'Her name is Sister Georgette. After she talked to your father, she called me into the room, and your Dad said that Sister Georgette said it was OK to cry. We cried like babies,' my mother said, beginning to cry again.

'Oh Mom, that's really wonderful.'

'I've never seen your father cry.'

'But Mom, you cry all the time.'

'I know how to work my upper lip.'

'You're the Princess of Pout.'

'But this is different.'

'I know it is. You mean you've never, ever seen him cry?'

'Never.'

In the following weeks, Dad began to slide into places where no one could be sure of his whereabouts. He had begun to take methadone as a pain killer. But he was annoyed by not being his usual sharp self, so he quit taking it. It was awful to see him struggling with his pain because he was trying to be the same person he had always been. He didn't want to live or die in a drugged state of mind.

I had grown up in a world of hashish, mushrooms, LSD and cocaine, and couldn't quite understand this revulsion my father had for finding himself in a drug-induced state of mind. He had a medically prescribed bottle of industrial-strength, goverment-approved marijuana in his medicine cabinet and he didn't want it. He had methadone to take the pain away, and he hated it. It had taken me years of trying everything voluntarily to decide that I didn't want or need to take the designer drug of the moment. But I was surrounded by a counter-culture that applauded what were thought to be 'pioneering' sallies into mind- expanding 'realities' that exposed day to-day perception as a shallow fraud. I went tripping voluntarily, and I wasn't on my death bed.

A good pipe filled with aromatic tobacco, a well-mixed Manhattan with marmalade, these were drugs my father was friendly with. They were familiar to him, as familiar as his favorite chair, or his cufflinks/collar box. Methadone and marijuana were possibly as frightening as death to him, because when he was on them, he was on death's doorstep.

There were three links from my father's watch, carefully wrapped in paper in the cufflinks/collar box. My brother had no doubt put them there where they had remained, as though Dad might regain his strength one day, get out of bed, go on down to the jeweler and have the links put back in the watchband.

I had planned to see Dad on a Saturday, but Mom called on Thursday.

'Your Dad is really in a bad way. Can you come at once?'

When I arrived, Mom told me she thought it was time to take Dad to the hospital. I walked into the bedroom. My father looked terribly thin and small in the King-size bed. I sat down on the bed.

'How is it Dad?'

'Not too good.'

Mom had followed me into the room.

'I think it's time,' she said.

My father looked at me. It was the first time in my life I had ever seen fear in his face.

'We have to take you to the hospital,' my mother said.

My father nodded.

'All set, Dad? I'll carry you out to the car. Just put your arms around my shoulders.'

As I began to lift him, I realized he was holding on to the bedsheets.

'I don't want to go,' he pleaded.

I put him back down.

'You don't have to go if you don't want to. I won't make you do anything you don't want to do.'

'Oh Daddy,' my father moaned, 'I keep thinking about my Daddy.'

Hearing my father cry out for his father was like finding myself in an earthquake. We were all thrown to another emotional level. He started crying. I began to cry. My Mom, who could cry about anything, wasn't crying. I was now holding my father in the first real embrace we had ever shared.

'I love you Dad.'

'I love you too,' he cried in an anguished voice.

It was a desperate, loud declaration, like a man might scream 'I'm drowning, I'm drowning.'

'I wanted to hold my Daddy when he died,' he said, 'Oh Daddy.'

96

'It's time to go,' my mother said again, unable to stand the sudden unraveling of a lifetime.

I looked at my father.

'Let's just talk for awhile,' I said.

He gazed at me for the longest time.

'Your mother is right,' he finally said.

'Are you sure?'

'I'm ready.'

I lifted him out of bed. He was light as a child but I had never carried a heavier burden. He had carried me in so many ways for much of my life. Now it was my turn to carry him.

When we got to the hospital, an attendant brought out a wheelchair. As I wheeled my father into the lobby, he leaned toward me.

'I have to pee,' he said.

'Do you want some help?'

'That depends on who does the helping,' he said with a grin.

My father was back in command. That flash of humor at death's door was to me an amazing show of grace under fire. Once he was found a bed and all tucked in, he raised his arm to grasp my hand. He was going to shake my hand goodbye.

'Dad, I want to stay here with you.'

'What, and sit here 'till morning? No, you take your mother home. And promise me you'll look after her.'

'You know I will.'

'I know. It makes all of this easier. Anyway, I'll see you tomorrow, won't I?'

'You couldn't keep me away.'

We were still holding hands. My Dad squeezed my fingers in a long goodbye. I was unable to see the obvious. I didn't want to know I would never see him alive again.

TRANCE TALK

'Remember me? I came to see you for a massage six months ago after having a seizure ...'

'Yes, I do remember. But why are you holding your hand that way?'

She was lying on her back on the massage table, her right arm snuggled up to her side. Her hand was rolled over backwards like an Egyptian dancer. It was a decidedly spastic posture. She moved her hand to a more natural position.

'Oh, that's how it goes when I have seizures.'

'Will you move your hand back to that position?'

She did.

'How does your head go when you have a seizure?'

She looked back over her right shoulder, then returned her head to a normal position.

'No, keep your head in the seizure posture.'

'I can't. I feel like a geek.'

'Sure you can. Go ahead. Good! Now, what about the rest of your body? Where do the legs go when you have a seizure?'

She laughed out of nervousness I guess, and drew her knees up to the left until her posture was a contralateral contortion. Her knees were bent in one direction and her upper body arched in opposition. I stroked her hair like I was calming my cat. Her eyes glazed, and she fell into a trance state.

'This is weird,' she said, talking to herself more than me.

98

Her voice was slow and thick; formulating the simple sentence as though she were slightly drunk and happy.

I kept stroking her hair because it seemed right.

My mother stroked my hair when I was young and I always found it soothing. Many mothers brush their daughter's hair. There are nearly always positive associations to touching hair. Among men of all ages, a trip to the barber shop is one of the most delightful sensual experiences of life. Ever notice how men in barber chairs have their eyes closed so much of the time? The touch of hands and electric clippers around the ears, the talc and the brushing with ultra-soft animal hair brushes, all alter consciousness. Having your hair touched in a socially acceptable context is nearly always an experience that carries some trance regression since mothers do tend to play with our hair so much when we're children.

'When I lie with my arm like this, it feels dead,' she said.

But she didn't move her arm and she remained in her dreamy state.

'But your arm isn't changing color, so we know the blood is still circulating through it. What do you mean, when you say dead?'

'Just dead,' she said.

'Really? Well, let's imagine your arm really is dead. Are you willing to let it be dead? Just dead - all the way dead - right now?'

She closed her eyes and began some internal scanning.

'That's funny,' she said, when I imagine that, it feels better.'

'That is funny,' I said. 'That it feels better when you imagine it dead.'

Her eyes stayed closed. She didn't move.

'By the way, what should I do if you have a seizure?'

'Put a pillow under my head and just ... wait until it's over.'

I got a pillow and put it under her head.

'Let's go for it,' I said.

'What?'

'See if you can have a seizure.'

'I can't just have a seizure.'

'Maybe you can, how do you know? Have you ever tried? I bet you've never even tried! Hey listen, I've never seen a seizure. I'd like to see one. What do they look like?'

'My teeth chatter. I shake and jerk.'

'And lose consciousness?'

'Sometimes. Sometimes I don't.'

'Well, imagine you feel one coming on. Just a little one, don't go Grande Mall on me.'

'But I'm on medication to short circuit my brain so I won't have them.'

'Oh, the old Indian short circuit trick. Does the medication work?'

'No. It just makes me sleep twelve hours a day. I had nine seizures over the fourth of July weekend.'

'Jeeze, a record. I'm only asking for one.'

'You're funny,' she laughed.

'I know, so why not humor me?'

'My boyfriend hates it when I have them.'

'Your boyfriend?'

'It's the strangest relationship I've ever been in.'

'What's he like?'

'He's Oriental.'

I remembered her use of the word 'geek', referring to how she felt getting into her seizure posture.

'Chinese?'

'Japanese. He moved in to help me after the stroke, and things just happened.'

'They usually do when people move in. I wish I could get some-body to move in, but nobody wants to move in. I'd move in myself if I knew somebody with a serious seizure problem.'

She laughed. I was being flip and facile on purpose.

'Is your boyfriend supportive?'

'Well, no. He just wants me to get better.'

'I see your point. It would be much better if he wanted you to get worse.'

100

'You know what I mean.'

'I think so. But aren't you ready to get better yet?'

'Of course I am, but ... I guess I brought it on myself.'

'What do you mean?'

'Well, I was a workaholic and I smoked a lot.'

'Do you still smoke?'

She grinned. The small beginnings of a sneer crept up on her mouth.

'I smoke half a cigarette a day.'

'Why not smoke the whole thing?'

She laughed again.

'I'll tell you what,' I said, 'I'll take care of you for a week.'

'You will?'

'Sure. But bring your own cigarettes, and be prepared to try really hard to beat your old record of nine seizures in a weekend.'

'You really are funny.'

'Not at all. You did say you've been a compulsive person, didn't you? A workaholic? Why not drop your medication and see what happens, since it isn't working anyway?'

'Are you serious?'

'Not completely. You would have to talk to your doctor about that. But I remember how frightened you seemed when I first saw you so many months ago.'

'After seeing you, my doctor increased my seizure medication. One night I went into convulsions for six hours. When I came out of it I was in the hospital.'

'That must have been terrifying.'

'You know, until you asked me to try and have a seizure, I would have said I wasn't scared of them.'

'Maybe you just haven't been able to admit how frightened they make you. Maybe you've approached the seizures like a workaholic prizefighter. You seem to be shadowboxing with yourself and you can't knock out your shadow. What's the use in fighting with yourself? When I saw your hand in a seizure posture, I knew something *in you wanted to move toward your seizures. That's why I asked you to amplify the posture you were already showing me. I didn't know where it would go. It didn't matter whether I knew or not, because your body certainly knew. Why not try a new attitude toward your seizures? Why struggle against them? Try treating them like friends who are offering you information you need to know. Try giving up the struggle.'*

I moved to her feet and continued the massage. I had been stroking her hair and talking to her for half an hour or more. We parted with warm affection after the massage and she tipped me over 20%.

Almost a year later she was again on my table.

'How has it been for you? I've thought of you, and wondered whether the situation with your seizures has improved.'

'After seeing you my doctor again increased my medication dose. I went into convulsions again. When I came out of it I was again in the hospital. I told him I wanted to be taken off the medication, but he refused. Three doctors in that hospital agreed with him. They told me if they took me off the medication it might be fatal. None of them wanted that on their records. I probably would have died too, if I was taken off the medication all at once. Finally I found a general practitioner outside the hospital who was willing. He withdrew me from the medication very, very slowly, and I've been fine ever since.'

'How did you find the courage to make that decision when the stakes were so high?'

'I just knew inside myself that I wasn't that weak. I had two weeks of lying in the hospital to think about it.'

'And since then?'

'No seizures.'

'None?'

'Not even one.'

'That's wonderful, really, really wonderful.'

102

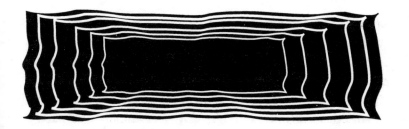

BLACKOUT

When the lights went out, I had just put my hands on the man. I had never given him a massage before and we were plunged into darkness. I traced my hands down to the side of his head, but continued to touch his temples. It's supposed to be good form not to 'break contact' with someone while giving a massage. In school we laughed about not taking a chance on causing anybody any separation anxiety. I don't worry about it since I'm convinced I'm connected with the person I'm working with even if I'm not touching them every moment. But this was different. Taking my hands away would have been like losing my roadmap.

'Must be having some trouble with the lights,' I said.

'It's really blowing out. Maybe the lines are down.'

'We often wore blindfolds in massage school to increase our sensitivity, but this is blackness. Maybe the lights will come on in a few minutes.'

The massage room in the club was beneath street level. There weren't any windows and everything electrical in the club had abruptly ceased to be electrical. The heat pump for the jacuzzis was no longer pumping. Only the battery clock was still ticking. I could hear a few voices in the men's and women's locker rooms, but they quickly faded away and we were left with the darkness and silence.

In the darkness, I thought I could see the electricity produced by my body. Even though there was no light, there were specks of light when I closed my eyes. Do the eyes see 'remembered' light? Is this an optical illusion? Does the brain start producing fireworks when somebody cuts the lights? No, doctor, I can't read the eye chart, but I do see the Roman Candles.

It was an unusual situation but the sudden darkness was a lift. It was like this man and I were suddenly plunged into a sensory deprivation tank together, with nothing but my hands and his skin to tell us what was going on. The intimacy factor was shoved up several notches.

I wondered how I would know when to finish the massage. In any given hour, I might consult the clock as a reference point on where I was relative to how much time I had left. So many minutes for a head and neck, for instance. Hands and arms times two, maybe twenty minutes. Five minutes each foot. Ten for the backs of the legs. Say twenty for the back. Something like that. It often changed, depending on what seemed to be needed. How many massages had I given? Three thousand? Six thousand? I decided to trust my hands to know when it was time to stop.

'Should I continue?'

'By all means. I really need this massage.'

'What's going on?'

'Too much. The worst of it is, a friend just died of AIDS.'

'No wonder you're stressed.'

'I've been sick myself for weeks. Last week I was sure I had AIDS too when I got a rash on my chest.'

A power surge suddenly rushed up my spine, causing a rush that registered in the hair shafts of my head. If the lights had been on, I might have removed my hands.

'What did your doctor say?'

'He said I had a rash on my chest. Gave me some cortisone cream to put on it. It's gone away, but I was in a panic for days.'

'Have you taken the test for AIDS?'

'No.'

'Why not?'

104

'There's a general feeling in the gay community that getting tested isn't a good idea.'

'Really? Why not?.'

'If you test positive, you're likely to scare yourself so bad you'll undermine your immune system. Anyway, there's nothing you can do. Or you test negative, which doesn't mean a thing since it can take years for the virus to show itself.'

'Did you know that the state now requires anyone licensed in the helping professions to take an AIDS training seminar? If you test positive there are medications that can slow the effects of the disease. And if you test negative, I bet you it would mean something to you.'

It was a good thing Mr. Knowledge showed up at that particular moment, because Mr. Scaredy Pants was in danger of taking over. It was one thing to sit in class and be told there was no possible way to contract AIDS by touching someone; that the mixing of bodily fluids and only the mixing of bodily fluids could provide the cruel little beggars a water passage between bodies. It was quite another thing to be touching someone in the dark without being able to see if your hands were about to move into a liquid lesion.

When I felt finished with the massage, I thanked my client and moved to the door like a sleep walker with outstretched hands. As soon as I opened the door, I could see candlelight. It had been an hour exactly. Staff members had placed candles on stools throughout the men's locker room, but nobody was around. I held the door open and my client got up and walked by me, stopping au naturale before me.

'That was so great. I would like to come to you for massage every week if I could?'

'Certainly. Though I can't promise darkness every time.'

Mr. Smooth had appeared when I least needed him. What I wanted to say was 'Every week. Wow, I'll have to think it over. Sure, I've taken the AIDS training, but I can't say I'm totally without concern, here.' Instead I just looked at him, my false face *warmly joining in the charade.*

This was one time I had misplaced my hands. My massage had become a matter of friction; combustion produced by a tissue abrasion between my palms and his tissue.

When I told them about this session, three of my co-workers said they wouldn't want to see the man again. Why risk it, was the consensus of opinon. Thinking about my reservations, I realized they were all based on fear, rather than factual information. Was I a healer, or merely someone who practiced massage? Was I even capable of working with him without having my objections get in the way?

There were thirty students in my massage graduation class. Two of us were men. I remember hoping at the time that I might get lucky and never have to give the other guy a massage. But every student had to give every other student a massage. And getting a massage from this male student, I discovered that it was good to be touched by another man. Touch between men is so taboo in North America and the fear of homosexuality so prevalent, that the lack of male touch is a deprivation we don't even allow ourselves to acknowledge.

When I was seventeen I ran away from home. I was hitchhiking when a gay predator stopped to offer me a ride. When I told him I was running away, he was all reasonable concern. He worried about how hard it would be for my mother when she discovered I was gone. Had I left her a note? Did I have enough money to make it to California? Was there somewhere I could stay when I got there? He convinced me I ought to think it over rather than go off half-cocked. Looking back on it, I don't think buying a case of beer and taking me to a drive-in movie so we could have time to 'think it over rationally' was the act of a truly concerned person. I drank beer until I threw up and passed out. When I woke up, I was in a motel room with him attempting oral sex with me. I swung on him and though I missed, he very quickly left the motel room.

I had to try and figure out where I was and hitchhike back home with a horrendous hangover headache.

Fortunately or unfortunately, depending on whether you take a long view or a short view, my mother had suffered a complete vodka black out herself the night before and never knew I had left the house.

Finding myself in such a situation was so shocking that I developed a black out myself for that memory and never discovered it again until I found myself giving a gay man a massage in the dark. I wonder how that forgotten memory has changed my life? I've lived so much of my life in the dark. Which probably, I would guess, isn't really so unusual.

That experience in the motel room, though it wasn't a conscious memory at the time, probably made it even more difficult for me to become comfortable with giving men who were obviously gay, a massage. But year by year I discovered that gay men were no threat to me. My gay clients were thoughtful people who brought lively intelligence and humor to our sessions. I was never overtly approached, and I even wonder whether my being so obviously 'straight' allowed them to more fully relax.

Often I worked with clients at my apartment. One gay man, a client of many years, once brought flowers and a bottle of wine to his session. It didn't occur to me until after he had gone home that he might have hoped I would invite him to have a glass of wine when the massage was over.

After pondering over the man who was worried he might have AIDS for days, I could see no reason not to accept him as a client. My hesitations were based on groundless fears, and I was especially reluctant to let fear become a factor in any of my decisions.

He became a weekly client and remained a weekly client for three years.

Once, when he got off the table, he said:

'Coming to you for massage means so much to me,' and impulsively gave me a hug.

Being hugged, however briefly by a naked man was a startling experience. For my part, I was understandably unable to return the hug.

In time this client invited me to parties, bought me gifts and sent me Christmas greetings. He had a longtime life partner, and I never felt that these 'attentions' were unwelcome or involved any subtrafuge, though gifts rather than gratuities, do signify something more personal.

I've been asked whether tips are appropriate for massage. It depends on the massage and the 'arrangement' the massage therapist has with the place where he or she works. Sometimes the person giving the massage is already well paid. But since there's no industry standard, agreements can vary greatly.

It's always OK to ask what the arrangement is and base your decision on the answer you recieve.

Myself, I'm particularly fond of impulse tippers.

TANGELO

'My body is singing!' she said.

I noticed the tangelo where I had left it on the table, cradled in its own peeling, the orange of it peeking through the soft white webbing. I had eaten several segments and forgotten about it.

Christine and I got wrapped up in planning the massage, then our client came and I forgot the fruit was on the table, half eaten, pregnant with pungent juice. The fragrance rose to the corrugated styrofoam squares in the ceiling above us.

'This is absolutely the greatest,' said our mutual client.

Outside, there were still patches of snow on the ground, residual white reminders of the startling, wind-whipped wonderland that had swirled in the week before, riding a freezing ridge out of Alaska.

The water pipes at the beach house had frozen with a slow motion liquid expansion, crystal by crystal, until the copper was torn asunder by the pressure.

'This is heaven! When I get to heaven, this is what I'll ask for.'

I wasn't looking forward to lying under the beach house, the cold, wet sand on my back, trying to fix the broken copper pipes. It takes hours to dig yourself a burrow under the house. Even with the shovel handle cut in half so it won't bang against the floorboards. It's digging lying down. Sand gets in your hair and down your boots and your pants get wet. Lying beneath the breaks in the line, having waved away the spider webs, having noticed the pale orange cocoons nesting in the dark corners (precious eggs of progeny), hav-

ing wiggled your way in like a snake, you prepare to light the torch.
In your pockets you carry the matches and flux and solder. You
bury the flashlight in the sand at just the right angle to illuminate
the work. You're squinting ...

Sand fleas do not consider this a tight situation. They bound
about with abandon, like teenagers playing volleyball on the beach.

Best to keep your mouth shut and try to light the torch, which
never lights easily. Up close it sounds (when lit) like a passing jet
plane.

I brought my attention back to the massage at hand.

Our client was so much more than a client. She had been a
fortnightly recipient of massage for five years. She was my unoffi-
cial counselor. She was a trial attorney with a big heart. She had
paid for an ad I ran in the 'personals' of Seattle's young professionals publication, The Weekly. She helped me write the ad from a
woman's perspective. She had given both Christine and I money
when she knew we needed it. In my case three hundred dollars.

She was always cold. A blanket and a heating pad were standard issue when she got a massage. A hot water bottle would
have been welcome. She wouldn't have complained if you stuck
two hot rocks under her feet. She was, as they say in boxing
circles, 'in my corner'. Out of gratitude, though the ad had not
produced a woman who was right for me, I had insisted on giving
her three ninety minute massages.

She came once a week for massage, alternating between coming to me and coming to Christine. It occured to me I could give
the 'gratitude' massages on Christine's time, so I wouldn't have to
block out the time on my schedule. Christine was all for it. Doing
a 'four hands' massage was something we had talked about, anyway. The sessions, like the Tangelo, would have segments, and we
were doing the second of three segments.

The first session had been wonderful. It was a festival atmosphere. We were all laughing a lot, and Christine and I both enjoyed the chance to look across the table while we worked and see

110

each other there. Massage is in many ways a solitary occupation. We hook ourselves to our clients in psychic and physical ways, but they often disappear into territories and terrain we can't share. We often find ourselves standing alone, working hard, with nobody to talk to.

At the best of times, we could break into song when we see our favorite clients coming. Sometimes we wish we could get on the table ourselves. And when we feel like that, the dialogue might go something like this:

'I'm so utterly glad to see you! You can't imagine the hell I've been through this week. My previous client was a brick wall with a bank account. An iron and bolts android form Andromeda. The pipes have burst, my cat is a flea farm, I got rear-ended by a guy with no insurance and I'm totally whacked out! You don't mind if I get on the table instead of you today, do you?'

The client we were working with had always bent over backwards for me. Sometimes I would be giving her a massage, but she was metaphorically on the floor, attempting to do the 'limbo' under a bamboo pole (the gnarly symbol of my current problem), while I gave myself sincere deep tissue work in my abdominal region. I think of regular clients as patrons since their patronage makes my existence so much more comfortable in every way. Most of us live our lives without ever being touched simultaneously by more than one person. Many seminars in the 'human potential movement' use multiple touch to produce memorable bonding moments. I really wanted to give this woman a memorable experience.

In the first session, I asked her to think about the session in the coming week and give us suggestions in the following week. It was a suggestion that could only help her relax during the week, and it would offer us a guide on how to proceed the second time.

'Did you think about the massage during the week?' I asked while we were working on her the second time.

'I dreamed about it,' she said. 'I told two friends about it. My husband just laughed, because he knows how much I love massage.

Sometimes it felt awkward when you were both working on my hands. It seemed to be smoother when you were working contralaterally.'

'Contralaterally?' Christine said.

'When Michael was working on my right arm and you were working on my left leg. Maybe it was just that you were doing slightly different things on my hands at the same time.'

'That makes sense. There are so many sensory receptors in the hands, I imagine it jams the neural pathways to have so many conflicting signals trying to cross the interstate all at once.'

'Other than that, everything worked wonderfully. Sometimes I wasn't sure whose hands were where. You two are so complementary.'

The third session - we had all agreed - would be a completely silent session.

But the snow threw a wrench into our plans. The temperatures rose, the pipes thawed, and suddenly there was water gushing against the bottom of the beach house. I canceled the third session so I could fix the pipes. I thought the thaw might actually be a helpful caprice on Mother Nature's part, since it would only add to the anticipation our client would have. She would have an extra week to add to the charge of her anticipation.

I was looking forward to that session and the silent delights it would bring. I was eager to see Christine's bright eyes in silence. It was a wonderful experience, rich in the hush of wordless tranquility and best left in the lavish realm of imagination.

TRANSIENT AUTHORITIES

He was thirty years old, heavily muscled, and wanted to know whether to lie face up or face down on the massage table.

'Face down,' I said.

Something about him made me nervous. Sometimes a case of nerves is contagious. I might feel nervous without being aware of the subtle inflection or gesture that infects me. Belly up is more vulnerable than face down. If he was nervous, he would feel more secure by beginning face down.

How carefully can an initial touch be made? With how much respect can one person enter another person's world?

As my hands settled on his back, and my fingers fanned out across his tissue, his skin reacted as though his nervous system had gone into red alert. It was like looking down from a small aircraft and watching a sudden wind rush through a field of wheat. His goose bumps ran ahead of my hands like a startled herd of red antelopes. It was unusual, and I wondered what it could mean. I worked in silence as we got to know one another. After ten minutes, I asked if he'd ever had a massage before.

'Not by a professional,' he said.

While working with him, his back began to soften. I applied my elbow along his long back muscles, sinking in gradually, coaching him to breathe and slowly increasing pressure. When I felt near the limits of his tolerance, I held the pressure.

'What kind of work do you do?' I asked.

'I'm a policeman.'

I couldn't think of a thing to say. It was as though he had said he wasn't the same kind of human being I was, but one of a special species who had an extra pair of ears on his hips. I even experienced a momentary paranoia, realizing that I had broken the law in the past. My crimes were more like hairline fractures than actual breaks. But I had helped a friend steal a three-volume set of books from a bookstore in my college days by diverting the clerk into the rare books section. It was, in my mind, my most serious crime. We thought of ourselves as two starving writers conducting a literary emancipation, but we were just two young men trying a stupid thing. I had tried drugs and that too, was illegal. I pilfered a Milky Way and two Mars Bars in my youth.

These crimes against the state didn't flash through my mind as I worked on him. But I was definitely working 'on' him rather than 'with' him. It was a momentary alienation. The policeman was not like me. He was 'the other'. If I was black, he was white. If I was Christian, he was a Jew. If he was Chinese, I was Russian. Then I realized how crazy my momentary paranoia was.

'I was a sports policeman for awhile,' I said. 'I used to referee high school basketball games. People don't like you much when you're a referee. They ignore you, or they're glaring at you.'

'That's true.'

'Are you on the street?'

'In the street on a bicycle.'

'No kidding? You're on a bike all day?'

'That's right.'

The bicycle police in Seattle have become so successful that bicycle police were now being tried all over the country. They wore bright yellow rain jackets of light-weight Gortex fabric. With white 'Gyro' crash helmets that have wide blue stripes down the middle. In the summer they wear shorts; carry short-wave radios on their gun belts. The weighty revolvers in the dark brown holsters give

114

the necessary air of authority, but the colorful uniforms made the law look like something cheerful, rather than something fearful.

'It sounds great,' I said, 'what's it like?'

'It's fun. And different. People who might never approach you if you're walking a beat, will talk to you when you're on a bike. I think it makes us less threatening.'

Sometimes people can be overwhelmed by massage. The richness of it, both physically and psychologically, is so total. They may have no way to fit it into an existing system of morals ('it's not right being touched by a stranger'), or some past thinking patterns ('massage is something sexual'), or they simply have no language to describe the fullness they felt. They may think other people will think them odd if they admit to having had a massage.

They may even hide the memory of how good it was, from themselves. When Paul was leaving the club after his massage, I saw him again at the reception desk. I started to say goodby to him but he looked away as if he hadn't noticed me. I thought it quite possible, even likely, that I wouldn't see him again. I remembered those goose bumps. I thought he might have found himself uncomfortable being touched by man. I assumed he had already buried his experience.

He surprised me by coming back for a massage the following week. His manner soon demonstrated to me that I had been guilty of stereotyping. Since he was a police officer, I assumed he might be lacking in sensitivity. In fact, I had been the insensitive one. It only occured to me much later that policeman carry the burden of our individual sins against society; that our crimes make them outcasts; that they pay with a very real social solitude, for the mistakes we make.

I learned in time that he had been named officer of the year by the Seattle Police Department. He had founded the bicycle mounted police, and now traveled all over the country helping other police departments organize their own bicycle police units.

We were talking about vacations once when he said he was planning a trip to Spain for a month.

'Why Spain?'

'To improve my Spanish.'

'Why Spanish?'

'So I can be more effective on the street.'

'You're so dedicated! That's great. Does the police department give you any financial aid for education?'

'No. They used to have a Spanish class at the station house, but they don't have it anymore.'

He had been riding a bike professionally for over a year. Eight hours a day, five days a week. He rode in races for the joy of it before it became a part of his job. The bottoms of his feet had thick callouses where his shoes met the pedals. His quadriceps, the driving force for his wheels, bulged away from his knees at an amazing angle.

As his confidence in me grew, he told me eventually that he was gay. And talked about the bias that caused him on the police force. I thought about my own unfortunate homosexual experience, and looking back on it, it seems to me I probably wouldn't have joined the Marine Corps if it weren't for that awful night. After that I needed to prove to myself I was all man. Although I never put the two things together at the time, they were probably connected.

After working as a massage therapist for many years, I now know that my clients are my teachers. They expand my understanding of the world and the people who populate it. Words which before were only job descriptions, flesh out, become reality soaked, become transformed into breathing, flesh and blood people. Understanding moves beyond caricature. In this way, strangers are in charge of my education. And my humanity is enlarged day in and day out, by transient authorities.

STIR UP THE MONKEYS

"How was our performance?"

Even after two grueling weeks in a hospital bed, Mom has hope. She's been told by her doctors that she has five, maybe six weeks to live. She has entertained a roomful of people, though it leaves her exhausted. It has been a courageous performance. The morphine solution has gone from 15 to 25 milograms. My brothers and I watch the nurses tend to her daily. I give her a foot massage and massage her hands. 'How was our performance?' is a phrase that comes from a courageous place in her that plays with the drama of the situation.

'You were magnificent!' I say. 'It's an Emmy! An Oscar!

'When will I see my doctor? Am I going home?'

'I'm not sure when they'll let you go. But we're working on it.'

At times, Mom seems happy, though she has a chest tube draining her right pleura sack. My younger brother, doing penance for ignoring her in the past, has been coming to the hospital every day. A parade of lifelong friends, also enter the room day by day. She likes the attention.

Mom can take liquids if we squirt them into her mouth with a syringe. She has made a joke of the syringe method, dubbing it 'The Hydra Ease Solution.'

'The Hydra Ease! It will make us all rich!' she says.

We never know what she's going to say next. She really seems to feel that people dying everywhere will be eased in their struggle by this technique. And maybe she's right, since swallowing is often nearly impossible in so many medical situations.

My older brother David, a retired Marine Corps colonel who has seen men die on the battlefield, isn't able to be in the room for ten minutes without crying. In war he had led a night ambush into enemy territory. His platoon destroyed a convoy. He was awarded the Silver Star. Ten men in his patrol died. When I asked him whether he ever grieved, he said he prayed, but didn't grieve.

'Did you grieve when you came home?' I asked.

'I never thought about it at all when I came home.'

I guessed that he was unable to grieve for his men since he was the officer in charge and could show no sign of weakness. Then he came home and I guess it didn't matter. Now the dam had burst. Seeing Mom dying he says to me, 'this is like combat duty.'

I want to take Mom home, but when the discharge nurse hooks us up with the hospice workers, the hospice workers say it will cost over a thousand dollars a day to take her home - given her present medication, and the care she needs.

'And if we take her to a nursing home?'

'It will all be paid for.'

When it was time to take Mom to the nursing home, I rode with her in the ambulance. The director of the nursing home asked me to sign a Power of Attorney agreement.

I had a Durable Power of Attorney form faxed to me by my mother's attorney. Since Mom had high blood pressure and was in danger of a stroke and a coma, Durable Power of Attorney was the only document that made sense. Power of Attorney means nothing if the subject of the document falls into a coma. Mom had suffered a small stroke, and she was in danger of falling into a coma.

Every day it was like trying to swim underwater. I was sleepwalking, but my brain was hyperactive. When I was given Durable Power of Attorney my head cleared. Legally I was now my mother's attorney.

118

My younger brother and I scouted out the nursing homes. The one we chose was the only one in the running, though we went to three places. We liked the people and the ambiance, though we knew it wouldn't be up to Mom's Architectural Digest standards. She was, as we had anticipated, less than enthusiastic.

'This just won't do,' she said, taking the highbrow approach.

But it had to do. It was the only place that would 'do', for every reason we could think of.

'Give it a try. It's only a transitional facility. We'll get you home, but first you have to eat and gain strength...'

We hadn't reckoned on Lief. Lief was a 'bed attendant' at the nursing home. He had a Scandinavian accent, a goatee, a nose ring, a lip ring and a large earring on his left ear. He seemed to me to be a gentle person, but his appearance totally unnerved Mom.

When I went to visit the next day, Mom claimed Lief had told her he loved her.

'He told me he loved me,' she said, 'I screamed for help.'

'But Mom, he didn't mean it in any evil way. He was probably trying to comfort you.'

'Where am I?'

Her question threw me out of sync. Did she really not know where she was? Was she playing on my sympathy? Had she decided to try on being pathetic, or was it the morphine talking?

'This is the nursing home, Mom. Don't worry, We'll be with you constantly.'

'Help! Help!'

'Mom?'

'No men! No men!'

'OK, Ok, no men. I didn't know you felt that way. I'll make sure Lief doesn't come into your room anymore.'

'Call 911! They're talking about Angels. They're giving me Angel dust and cocaine!'

'They wouldn't do that, Mom.'

'They did do it. This just won't do. It just won't do. Where am I?'

My younger brother came into the room.

'You're in a transitional health care facility,' I said. 'Take it easy, Mom, Steve is here.'

'Hi Mom.'

'Angel Dust and cocaine honey. They're giving me the drugs!'

'They are giving you drugs Mom, but it's only Morphine so you won't be in pain. We'll never get you out of here if you don't start eating. You've been two weeks without food! I brought you some soup. Sound good?'

'No.'

'Oh my gosh,' Steve said, 'I'm really relieved. They weighed you this morning and you were ninety three pounds. Ninety three pounds! We're going to put you on a diet!

'Oh all right, I'll have the soup.'

'Have you seen Lief? No wonder she's freaked out.'

'He's as nice as peaches! As pears!

My brother Steve always took the humorous approach.

'I know it. But he scares Mom. We've got to insist that no men attend to her.'

'They're talking about me like I'm not here again,' Mom said.

'No men! No men!' Steve teased.

'I want make-up,' Mom said.

Apparantly he had been standing in the hall and heard her cry out earlier.

'Make up?'

'It's in my overnight case.'

I got the case and opened it, then looked at my brother.

'Would you like to do this?'

'You did it in the hospital. How can I compete with Michael of Hollywood? Every woman wants to look like a woman in the morning. Unless they want to look like a man of course. In which case, why not give her a shave?'

'Don't be a pansy,' Mom said. 'Get out the eyebrow pencil and accentuate my eyebrows. But not too much!'

120

'Ooooh, nice work,' Steve teased as I stroked away with the eyebrow pencil.

'And now the eye shadow,' Mom demanded.

'Eye shadow?'

'The blue eye shadow. I'm feeling blue. Just find the brush, the blue color and do it.'

'Just do it! Hey, that could be a slogan,' Steve says.

I found the blue eye shadow. Mom always said she wanted to be surrounded by men, and that's why she had three boys. But she always wished she had a daughter. Fortunately, she had several substitute daughters. She was good company. She and her 'daughters' went out to lunch and talked regularly on the telephone. And visited daily now that she was confined to a bed.

In the courtyard, I talked to my brother Steve.

'I'm not ready to give up on Mom,' he said. 'I'm not convinced she's dying of cancer. But she may starve to death if we don't get the food down. We'll buy her a refrigerator! We'll get protein powder. She'll eat like she's never eaten!'

'I think they call this denial, Steve.'

'Hey, miracles happen all the time. Just keep that syringe full and make her eat her sorbet. Or maybe ice cream is the key. I'm praying for her. Prayer is powerful. I've seen miracles!'

That afternoon I got the new mini-refrigerator.

The diagnosis was metastatic lung cancer. I started smoking right away. I was like the Doctor in the Kafka story who wants to get in bed with his patient. It was for sure Mom was dying. Every doctor, every hospice nurse, prefaced their remarks with the opening statement, 'your mother is dying.' I didn't doubt it. After seeing my father die of cancer, I had taken a fourteen day death and dying seminar with a famous guru of how to be with the terminally ill.

Self mutilation was never mentioned, but I began to cut myself. Every day another small, accidental slice somewhere, as if to 'bleed' my body like they did in the medical dark ages. Maybe trying to cleanse the horror of what was happening. Or possibly to hurt myself and share the burden of pain.

Mom began to 'stir up the monkeys'. It was a phrase she often used. The monkeys were the men in her life. It was always easy for an attractive woman to stir up her own particular monkeys. When my older brother appeared she took his hand.

'Oh Dave, I know you of all people will understand,' she said, attempting to appeal to his vanity.

And told him about Lief. And how spooky it was in 'this place'. And would he please call the police?

The monkeys didn't stir. Mom would have to think of another way to make her break; the great escape from the 'Transitional' nursing home.

A year after my father died, Mom had fallen and broken her hip. She had to have hip replacement surgery. After the surgery, she couldn't move on the massage table with any ease. She had forgotten, if she ever knew, how to relax. She was medicating herself with box wine. She was often eager to have me finish the massage so she could get up and smoke. There was a modesty issue to work around. She was rigid, but playful. At first she thought massage was a game. It was like trying to give a massage to a giggling adolescent, trapped in an aging body.

I found her frustrating to work with but she thought I was the greatest thing since soapsuds. I was helping her 'immensely'. I was happy she thought so because what she thought about how she was doing was what mattered.

After she was walking more easily, she wanted to take me on a cruise. We could 'share a cabin'. A week or so on the Sea of Cortez.

'I wonder if we could share a cabin for a week and survive to talk about it,' I said.

'Sure,' she said. 'You'd be upstairs with the fun people, anyway. I'll send for some brochures.'

During the week, I shared what I saw as my dilemma, with one of my massage clients.

122

'Is it really so difficult between you and your mother?'

'Emotionally we're close, but her drinking and the physical and verbal tics of her habit drive me nuts. I begin to go crazy after about four hours of it. My younger brother only sees her a couple of times a year because of her drinking. My older brother usually visits in the late mornings to be on the safe side. I've been to Al-Anon and Alcoholic Anonymous meetings and I've discovered the best thing I can do is remove myself when she gets that way. Can you imagine sharing a cabin with that for a week? I'd jump overboard.'

'Why not tell her you'd love to go, on the condition that she doesn't drink?'

A brilliant idea!

When the brochures came, I told Mom my condition. Her expression went from resistant to amazed, to tearful.

'What are you thinking?' I asked.

'Lots of things.'

'Can you share them with me?'

'I'm not going to change at sixty seven,' she said, and defiantly made here way to the wine box.

In the following months, I confronted her several times more, talking to her about the things she did that bothered me when she was drinking. That she repeated herself when she was sober. How exasperating it sometimes was to be the son of two different mothers. Her reactions were always a rainbow of emotions, from anger to tears. She was a cagey maintenance drinker. She didn't drink before noon. She only drank box wine. She never drove at night. She wasn't an angry drunk. She was more likely to get playful and want everybody in a party spirit. She had an ample fixed income, so her drinking had no financial repercussions. Her drinking didn't get her into any outside trouble; it just meant she didn't see as much of her sons and her grandchildren.

My older brother David had been an alcohol abuse counselor in the Marine Corps. We considered confronting her as a family, but the fact that her drinking didn't really get her into any actual trouble *(it just made her occasionally silly and boring), and her advanced years, precluded any of us being able to vote to take that step. We had all known dry alcoholics who were ornery and unpleasant to be around. Finally, I decided to accept her as she was and continue to practice the alcoholic equivalent of defensive driving.*

The decision to accept her as she was made all the difference. I teased her about her drinking rather than reprimanding her, and she began to see her drinking self more clearly. I teased her about being controlling, and she began to notice when she was doing it. It became a game between us. She was more careful about her drinking, though there were still occasional lapses. We become friends, and over the next eight years the best of pals. I had finally come to know my mother as a friend. We found out that we were two adults who actually liked and appreciated each other.

And now I was losing her.

Steve humorously referred to our brother Dave as 'the crying colonel' one day. Dave has begun to refer to the nursing home as 'the nursery'. Unconsciously (I suppose), hoping Mom is in a place where something good can grow. And I'm cutting myself. But I'm proud of 'the crying colonel'. In my eyes a real man reveals by crying unguardèd tears. I'm proud of Steve, too; he spends fifteen hours with Mom one day, and is with her more than anyone else day to day. The crisis has drawn us together. Though we usually only see each other several times a year, we're now talking and planning daily.

One morning at three a.m., it's the telephone. The night nurse is telling me that 'your mother is demanding we call 911.' Mom wants to go back to the hospital. I dress and drive down to the nursing home.

'I have a right to call 911,' Mom says when I enter the room.

'Mom, I've talked to the nurse about it. Yes, you can have her call 911. But the emergency response team will only come and declare that this isn't an emergency. And you're right. You can demand an ambulance take you to the hospital. But you've already been discharged from the hospital. If we call an ambulance

124

to take you to the hospital you'll spend hours lying under fluorescent lights while they take care of the automobile accident victims and people with gunshot wounds. Then they'll look at you, discharge you again, and you'll be right back here.'

'Chicken feathers, I saw them. And you stole the earplug. I saw you put it in your pocket.'

'Oh Mom. Here, let me give you some sorbet.'

I get it out of the refrigerator. She takes a bite, then puts her finger in her mouth and takes it out, the sorbet dripping on her gown.

'Here's the proof! It's cocaine! Call 911!'

'Mom, mom, it's only sorbet and protein powder. Honey, please listen to me. I'm going to take you home, but be patient. It will cost a thousand dollars a day. A thousand dollars every day! Don't worry, we'll get you home somehow. But I have to tell you, if you insist on going back to the hospital tonight, I'm not going with you.'

'What about the earplug?'

'That's the morphine talking Mom. You're not used to it. It scares you, and makes you see things. I don't know why they don't have people explain the hallucinations to you when they give you this stuff. I'm sure it's terrifying, but we don't want you hurting. Just go with it; try not to let fear get a grip on you.'

'You're all trying to kill me!'

My father sometimes took a scornful tone of voice with Mom when she was drinking too much. He would send her to bed like she was a naughty child. I tried the scornful approach.

'Listen, young lady. If you want to die thinking everybody is trying to kill you, that's your choice! We're doing all we can do. You get some sleep! I'll see you tomorrow.'

I wasn't good at being hard-nosed. I couldn't sleep any more that night. The next day I talked to Dave about it.

'She's so brave with everyone else,' I said. 'I mean she jokes and she's alert. But when they leave she's exhausted. And when I'm alone with her she doesn't pretend. She thinks I'm trying to kill her.'

'It's because she loves you the most that she blames you the most,' Dave said.

Mom hadn't let me touch her for several days. She didn't want any massage. That afternoon she asked me to rub her feet. She was suddenly on her best behavior. She asked me to give her several hundred dollars so she could tip the bed attendants. She wanted to send Steve and his family to Disneyland. I was to buy a new car.

She had begun to lose control of her bowel and she was embarrassed. The first time I changed her bed, I said 'I wet my bed 'till I was ten, remember Mom? You changed my bed so often, I could never catch up to you.'

'Payback,' she said.

My real Mom, the one with the sense of humor, was back. That afternoon when I went into the nursing home, the charge nurse informed me that Mom had asked to get up and 'meet some people'. They were getting her a wheelchair.

'Don't tell her I'm here. This I want to see.'

I followed my mother and the attendant down the hall, remaining behind her and out of sight. The first few 'people' she tried to meet had slipped into psychotic hiding places as a way to deal with the horror they found themselves undergoing. She might have done better to talk about the chicken feathers and the earplug. Finally, Mom did meet another lady in a wheelchair who was capable of a conversation. But the conversation was short and uninspired. Mom asked to be taken back to her bed.

I was like a proud parent. Her effort to adjust was so heroic. It was time to take her home.

The next day we removed Mom from the Infinite Vista nursing home. We put a hospital bed in her living room, so she could see her view of the mountains and water and so she would feel in the middle of things. I put two Chinese Foo Dogs on the table near her, as she had spent three years in China and knew the Foo dogs were meant to chase away evil spirits.

'Lights, camera, action!' she said, when we got her settled in.

The visitors began to knock on the door. My mother was well-loved. Among her visitors were teenagers whose parents didn't send them. They wanted to see her, as they had always wanted to see her. After she died, I got a card from a sixteen year old English-woman, the daughter of my friends, who had spent two weeks with my Mom at her beach cabin.

'Your Mom was truly a child among children,' she wrote. 'She accepted everybody as they were. She will be sorely missed.'

Mom lived another eight days at home. In the final days I gave up trying to massage her. Her tissue was too thin. She didn't have any muscle left. The hospice nurses who visited once a day to make sure the medication was adequate, advised us to stop feeding her or giving her any liquids. Experience had proven to them that dying by dehydration is a more comfortable demise than bloating to death.

Mom couldn't talk for the last three days. I began to rest on the bed behind her, my chest just behind her head on the mattress, cheek to cheek with her, my arms around her, my hands gently resting on her upper rib cage. On her final day I was holding her this way, and began sobbing. After several minutes, I became aware that Mom was cooing at me. Her last act as a dying woman was to make reassuring sounds to comfort one of her sons.

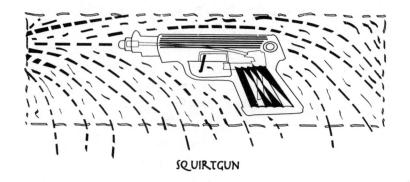

SQUIRTGUN

A year before my mother died intuition told me her health was failing, and I moved out of Seattle to be closer to her. She thought I needed a cat to keep me company. I wouldn't have gotten myself a cat, though I had found a cat for her eight years before. The cat I had given her we named Buffy. Buff was quite a character, and he was with my mother for eight years.

When my in-laws heard from my mother that I wanted a cat (which wasn't exactly true), they brought me a stray kitten. She was a Calico, maybe five weeks old. It appeared she had never been washed. When I gave her a bath and destroyed the flea circus she was supporting, I discovered she was white, with brown and grey patches.

I call her Meg, short for megabytes, since she generally sleeps on my computer. I also call her Maggie Bites because she does have that tendency. Sometimes I tag her 'Boodle Butt', since she has a unique way of walking. Meg isn't terribly fast, and doesn't seem particularly bright. She's clearly something of an odd duck. She has the softest, medium length fur coat, and she's quite independant. She wants everything her way no matter what. Talks with Maggie are therapeutic for me, but otherwise fruitless. If fruitful means Maggie is going to pay attention to what I want, then yes, there will be no bananas.

Even when I mention the decline of cats in Cuba (where people are so meat-hungry that cats were no longer seen in the streets of

Havana), there is no obvious impact. Meg isn't worried that she might end up as say, roasted megabytes.

She's the only cat I've ever seen that gallops like a show pony. She kind of throws her front and back paws out like there's a panel of judges watching. She swings her hips with an attitude, attempting, always attempting, to lead me to the kitchen.

'If you only knew how lucky you are to have a babe like me around the house,' she seems to say, ' you would follow me all the way to Alaska, and produce (provided you were a real man), a plate of steaming shrimp on a bed of shelled crab legs.'

Why is she so fascinated when I'm doing my business? How come she can't let me sit in peaceful solitude? In the animal kingdom, consulting with the tail end is the first order of business, I guess. But what if people acted like that? It's the same old story every time. Within minutes, Maggie is on my lap. She can be sleeping in a closet somewhere and yet as soon as I got situated on the porcelain, she comes running.

She has designs on the toilet paper. One day she took off with the paper between her teeth and ran away with the entire roll, which was consequently stretched throughout the house in a mega-flash. It was her finest moment, and she's been trying to duplicate it ever since. There was nothing for it but to drive a nail into the wall as far up as I could reach, and hang the coveted object beyond her reach. She continues to gaze intently at it every time she approaches the throne, and once in a while I give her a few squares in an attempt at diplomacy. Give Maggie a couple of squares of toilet paper and her motor runs like it's flushing the finest oil.

I'm a neat person but I don't dust for months on end. It was lucky I found a housekeeper willing to trade her housekeeping services for massage. I soon discovered I wasn't keeping things in their proper places. I would reach for the spatula, and it was gone. Gone! It would take me a long time to find whatever was missing after my housekeeper decided it made more sense for me to keep it somewhere else. OK, maybe she's right. She's a woman after all, and

129

women often seem to know things I've never had an inkling about. So I give her the benefit of the doubt. After a month my house is totally re-organized. I have trouble finding anything at first, but I adjust.

Then the housekeeper starts working on me directly.

'You need another kitten,' she says.

'Otherwise, how will Maggie know how to act with other cats?

'Anyway,' she concludes, 'Maggie needs another kitten to keep her company.'

The conversation was finished, though I hadn't said a word.

So I soon found myself at the pound, saving another little Sheila. Taking another pitiful little face home so I can spend even more time scooping steaming chocolate colored rolls out of a litter box.

When I bring home the new charge, the first charge chases the second charge around, biting her constantly and in general, running down her wardrobe. Sort of a territorial deal, I think.

The new kid on the carpet won't eat, so I call her Anna Rex. Poor baby is torn up to be taken from her brood, though they did tell me at the animal shelter she wasn't too young to take . It wasn't until the third day that Anna Rex began eating.

In two weeks 'the girls' had begun to bond, and began comforting one another, since they could see at once that they were both prisoners of a rather gigantic tyrant. They started playing catch me if-you-can, cleaning each other, sleeping together, and in general, began to act like a couple of lesbians.

My ex-wife tried out the forbidden lifestyle of same sex-sex, and so did a woman I lived with for six years. I suppose same sex-sex, is only sex after all, but it sure messes with your mind and brings the axe right down on a relationship. The idea of same sex-sex still kind of spooks me. When the woman I've been having sex with decides to have sex with someone else of her same sex; it's like I'm stepping on an emotional landmine.

The antics of Maggie and Annie really didn't bother me, since they weren't actually having sex, but only acting like they probably would if they ever found out what it was. I had them fixed as the vet recommended.

Before breakfast, Maggie purrs, Annie hollers like a fishwife and these are, (as near as I can determine), their basic philosophies. So I get out of bed, walk to the kitchen and there they are under foot, trying to get me to accidentally kick them, so they can claim abuse.

'Can't you see I'm starving' seems to be Annie's song, and Maggie just stares at me intently.

The first month I fed them something my housekeeper referred to when she saw it, as 'Kitty Heroin' . Kitty Heroin is about nine hundred dollars a can and 90% water. The housekeeper immediately landed on my mistake, observing that Kitty Heroin seemed to make addicts of the best of cats. The girls didn't seem to care that the can was the circumference of a silver dollar because it apparantly had real chunks of the Golden Triangle in it. No matter how much dry food I put in front of them, they screamed for the Kitty Heroin.

The screaming in the morning kind of annoyed me, so I switched to Showy Banquet, which seems to be Mississippi mud mixed with a really ripe Tennessee terricloth. That's when Anna started heaving and hurling and I began to think of her as Princess Rex.

Pet names come to me without thought usually, and often make no sense. Kitty Buckets, Tittens, Chirpies, Noodlenoses, Poodle Berries, Spooky Spooks, Crab Bait, Squirrels and Doodledrops, for instance.

My training system, included hydratherapy with a squirtgun. There's nothing like hydratherapy to sedate the owner and chastise the cat. Squirtguns are great therapy for humans when aimed at a cat. There's something really, really satisfying about dowsing the girls when they misbehave, as they leave the room at warp speed. And they do hate to get wet.

When I'm hurting, I get wet myself, most commonly with frozen water. I use ice in spite of my discomfort because ice brings about miraculous changes in the body. Got hemmorhoids? Ever thought of ice? Kind of a startling thought, isn't it? It isn't as uncomfortable as you might imagine. Ice causes contraction. The blood recedes into the body. As the body surface warms again, the movement of blood brings change. Circulation heals us. By icing the place that hurts, we're causing circulatory benefits. When ice touches us, the brain over-rides the pain signal system, so icing also tends to give temporary pain relief.

When I first tried to give Mom Buff when he was a kitten, her reaction was cold. I may as well have been offering her an ice treatment. She refused to take him.

So I kept him for six months. Then Mom began to ask me to bring him for visits. Eventually, she suggested I might want to leave him 'for a few days'. That's when I knew Buffy had a new home.

As a caretaker, I'm not my mother's equal. Annie is neurotic and can't get enough touch, and Meg doesn't like to be touched. She appreciates a bit of facial stroking, but if you touch her anywhere else she slinks off. You can't imagine how frustrating it is for a massage therapist to have a cat who doesn't like to be touched. I'm sure this is a peculiar form of torture devised for me by fate. I'm sure all parents often feel tortured by their offspring. If I had sprung any offspring myself, I somehow doubt that I would have ever become a massage therapist. I wouldn't have been able to afford to send them to college, I know that.

Squirtguns work because of pressure. Sometimes we do our very best work under pressure. I'm under pressure right now for instance, trying to justify this chapter about cats. I thought this book needed some serious levity here, since the previous chapter was no picnic. So here I am caught in a paragraph trying to say something profound about touching and pressure and squirtguns.

What pressure is the best pressure? There's a tendancy among inexperienced massage therapists to equate deep-pressure work with good work. Sometimes massage therapists with the best intentions simply try too hard and apply too much pressure. No pressure is right for everybody, whether it's cats, egrets or elephants.

My father always said he wanted to come back as my mother's

cat. I was, in a way, one of my mother's cats, so I knew what he meant. As my mother's cat, I got strokes, and the very best food. After she died, I gave myself to my grief.

It took me months to really make a decision about Buff, who was being kept by my brother Dave, at my mother's townhouse. I already had two year old kittens to look after, so I was glad Dave could keep Buffy until the house sold. What would happen when the house did finally sell, wasn't talked about.

Buff acted strange from the time Mom went into the hospital. He was gone all day, and he didn't come into the house much after I brought Mom home to die. Of course, there was a lot of people coming and going. After Mom was gone, Dave would leave a bowl of dry food out for Buff in the morning and the food disappeared during the day, though he didn't know who was eating it. Buff had been taken off the Kitty Heroin cold turkey. All his usual routines were altered. He too, was in mourning.

One day a friend who worked for the city called to tell me Buff was showing up at the house of a colleague every morning for breakfast. They talked about it during a break in a meeting. Someone overhearing their conversation asked who Buffy was. Then the whole room had to hear about Buffy. It was suggested that Buffy be 'a line item' in the city budget.

This was good for a laugh, but Buff was now very much on my mind. I'm very fond of him, though I've always had to play the bad guy in his life. My agreement with my mother was that - if she took him - I would always be the one to take him to the vet for shots and such. Every Summer, then again in the Fall, I was the one who would transport him to and from the Beach house. He hated the car. Just hated it. He was a critter who didn't have a tendency to cozy up to any human beings, with my mother the provider the single exception. At eight years old, he was a middle aged cat.

Maybe Buff was even beyond the middle and somewhere on the final approach. This was possibly my own situation, though I did like to think the second fifty years would be an improvement on the first fifty. Who will take care of the old guys, like me and Buffy, I had to ask myself?

Two cats is a handful. Wouldn't three be a circus? Having a helping heart is good, but didn't one of these cats have to go? I can carry two bowls of food, but three bowls of food means two trips. Nevermind the extra trips to the vets and the upkeep expenses.

I had been in the helping profession for sixteen years, and just about worked out all my co-dependant issues. I see now that it was those issues that brought me to massage in the first place. Wanting to touch others was for me an attitude that had something to do with feeling out of touch with the world. I no longer needed to attempt being all things to everybody. It was an absurd notion in the first place; brought on by my own search for self-esteem.

Still, no harm, no foul. I had brought relief to many people. This work had given me a reason to be. It was good work, with rewards. Contact with hundreds of good people who never would have been a part of my life otherwise.

After thinking on it for several months, I knew letting any of the cats go, would have amounted to a hallow victory over what was left of my tendency to want to take care of everything. When I called to tell my brother I was coming to pick Buffy up, he told me Buff had been adopted the day before by the man who had jokingly suggested that Buff be a 'line-item' in the city budget. His six year old daughter had asked if they could keep him.

HOT LEMON WATER

I felt bloated like a Puffer fish. It was like I had swallowed an animal, one that continued to live inside me week after week, turning and twisting in my guts.

There were strange electrical occurrences in my apartment. The tape player and the radio tossed their functions back and forth, seeming to stage electrical anarchy against the programs determined by the amplifier. One day I was playing a tape when the radio came on. At the same time the taped music ceased - though the tape continued to transfer itself on the tiny plastic wheels - the radio music began. When I attempted to play the tape later, I discovered that the recorded music I was listening to had been taped over by the music that happened to be on the radio when the radio amplifier "turned itself" on. The warranty on my amplifier was still good, but after leaving the tape deck and amplifier at the dealer's service department for two weeks, it was returned with the comment that they could find nothing wrong with my equipment.

My television also began to fritz out on me, but it was an old black and white set, so I didn't think about it much until later. I took it to the local dump in a fairly cranky humor, and dropped it (from a height of 15 feet to the cement below), with some satisfaction.

The serviceman who checked out the amplifier did suggest that I could be in an unfortunate alignment with a radio tower that might possibly be interfering with my signals. So I began to suspect that this malfunctioning condition (of both my appliances and myself) might have something to do with an overabundance of man made electrical signals.

An electrical substation existed a block from my apartment, and I knew electrical power moves in a manner similar to water pressure. The closer you are to a substation, the higher the voltage will be in your house. There could be no doubt that I was living with a lot of voltage.

I had been diagnosed as having colitis, but the doctors couldn't supply me with a reason why I had contracted colitis. Essentially I had begun to bleed internally and nobody knew why. The inflamed distension of my colon was extremely uncomfortable. For someone who considers himself a healer, it's maddening to be sick without knowing why.

After awhile, I even wondered (reaching for every possible explanation) if the weird behavior of my electrical appliances might be a poltergeist effect I was somehow bringing on myself through strain.

One morning the winds woke me at daybreak, rattling my windows so violently I feared they might leave their glazed moorings. In the mirrored distortion of the billowing glass, I saw myself reflected by the erratic movements of the wind. It seemed like I was now stuck in a terrifying fun-house mirror.

The weather was in harmony with my dark mood, brought on by a month of being forced to examine the results of my internal, peristaltic movement. It was now a daily necessity, however revolting, to take note of the waste which my body didn't use as a way to track my condition.

Leaning over, staring into the gloss white toilet bowl, I was suddenly frozen and horrified. My stools were black.

Black!

Though I was told by my doctor to stay away from coffee, I longed for a cup of coffee. I think the longing had as much to do with implication, as residual addiction. If I was drinking coffee it would mean I was normal again; that the past was "on" again; that I could once again live my normal life with the common (and retrospectively delightful) cerebral worries of one healthy day after another.

In the previous three weeks I had seen a specialist and according to this man (a gastroenterologist), colitis could be caused by parasites (none were found), allergies (none that I knew of), cancer (not any that could be seen), even by emotions. There was no cure for colitis, only a treatment; the daily administration of sulfasalazine, a combination of sulfa and aspirin. This was to be taken "indefinitely" or until the symptoms subsided. The possible side effects for sulfasalazine in the Physician's Desk Reference ran to three pages. Sulfasalazine struck me as the Agent Orange of the antibiotic belly busters. Taking antibiotics indefinitely seemed to me the equivalent of napalming the intestines. I decided to seek a second opinion.

My allopathic doctors, members of the cooperative team of physicians where I had my health insurance, wouldn't cooperate. They simply ignored my request to send a copy of my records to a naturopath. Dr. A's position relative to my choice of seeking a naturopathic opinion, became clear when I asked if it would be possible to get a barium x-ray, a procedure which another doctor (a friend of a friend) indicated might be an excellent prophylactic measure.

'Well,' said Dr. A, 'you can choose this treatment or you can choose the naturopathic treatment, but you can't do both.'

I was caught in a war of dueling doctors. Dr. A was taking his marbles and heading home if I wouldn't play his way.

I went to see Dr. B., a naturopath. She suggested a cleansing diet, high in bulk fibers. With this approach there would also be a daily bombing run, only this time the bombs would be vitamins.

The gastroenterologist had recommended a white diet.

'Water chestnuts?' I had enquired.

'White Rice, potatoes, yogurt, cream, and hominy grits. Eat whatever is colorless and bland,' said Dr. A.

The naturopath believed "the white diet" would only make things worse.

At a prearranged appointment with the gastroenterologist the following day, he snorted when I told him I was going to go with the naturopathic treatment "to see how I respond". He spat out the word "vitamins" as though speaking of garden snakes he considered worthless, as they were without venom. He found it necessary to mention that my odds on cancer were one in three, "given your condition, in five to six years".

Though I knew I had colitis, there was a nasty intestinal flu going around and I was hopeful that this bug, from Hong Kong, Rangoon or wherever, was the reason I was feeling particularly bad on this windy, black bottom day. I was, in this odd way, wanting to believe that I had the flu.

With caffeine and alcohol taboo, I was drinking hot lemon water. Since I was supposed to get plenty of fiber, I was eating brown rice (rice cakes) for breakfast. The light as air chips of puffed rice were bouncing to the carpet as I broke them in lieu of bread, while gazing out my window.

Friends were withdrawing as my conversation was increasingly reduced to my condition. A few withdrew from the intensity of my worries as though I had shot my sleeves and revealed wrists that were eaten to the bone by leprosy.

So I began to fake a face on things.

The mortification of being a sick caretaker faking a face on things didn't help. My work as a massage practitioner now seemed to clearly indicate that I needed more practice. I cut my schedule to a few clients a day. Except for those few hours, my life was reduced to a contemplation of my breakdown. I felt that my problem should not have been posed in the first place, but the body that breathed me obviously didn't agree with my assessment.

My perplexity about why this sudden illness had come to me produced nothing but insufficient answers, and threw dark projections into what should have been common, everyday affairs. Future scenarios of even more difficulty were being slide-ruled into actuality by the weight of my daily worry. I was willing to try anything and everything to get well. In that regard, I was quite healthy.

In other ways, I was like meat spitting fat in an oily skillet. Like dipshit on the frying pan of frizzle. I was stranded in the cross fire of an invisible, ricochet zing-thing. It was like unseen and unknown electrical energies were playing my body like loud, careless children on off-key, honky-tonk pianos.

There had to be a very big (huge) problem with having that electrical power grid station a block away. All that unnatural electrical activity was obviously messing with my exquisitely normal bioelectric signals; shimmy-shaking the fine tuning of my interior electric lights and producing an internal lightening storm that had slowly, over the seven years I had lived there, turned me from jelly to jam.

In the oriental theory of organ energy meridian flow, it's common knowledge that the lung energy fuels and pushes the intestines, that the stomach fuels and nudges the spleen, that the spleen helps drive the heart and etcetera, each organ receiving energy, generating energy, and passing energy on through the living body.

My theory had it that the small intestine was a sausage-like generator coiling the electricity of the body (like any generator), but this generator wasn't just any generator, oh no. This generator was nothing less than the gathering place of living energy in the mortal coil. Basically, according to me, the small intestine was the crux of human existence, the core of continued creation, and probably our most vital organ. It wasn't much of a stretch for myself (the eminent "colonologist" of the renowned electrical sausage theory) to see that the intestines were susceptible (like the heart) to electrical interference.

Oh, these delicate ohms we weave.

The windows are no longer rattling. The wind has died down.

Beyond and below my window, Elliot Bay is in full bustle. A ferry comes to dock like a large white slug, cheerfully farting a melodious *low warning. Two tug boats hold steady offshore, waiting against the tide for a ship which is still only a speck below the pale outline of the Olympics. The mountains are barely visible through a morning gauze of distant sky. An overhead curtain of low hanging clouds squashes them into a narrow visual strip. Indistinct trees of the inland islands are made blue by space and reflection. Whitecaps still churn in the bay. A jumbo jet banks so low and slow it's difficult to understand why it doesn't fall like a stone to the water. A spot of blue sky exists to the south, but doesn't seem to be moving toward Seattle.*

My doorbell buzzes. I knew it was Annie, a colleague who agreed to come to my apartment to give me a massage, specifically a Trager treatment.

Trager work is a non-invasive, gentle rocking and rolling form of touch which at first may seem ineffective. But the nervous system is lulled into releasing the muscles by the gentle rotations. Muscle habits (habits of tension habitually held) often melt away with the extremely pleasant monotony of the hypnotic movement.

The light compassion of Annie's touch as she began her treatment, seemed to telegraph all the empathy she felt for my situation, which she knew about, being a friend. I felt enfolded in soft concern. It was like I was a mummy long calcified; as if she was slowly unraveling the layers of my constriction. My body became lighter as I sunk more deeply into the soft table over time. When she placed her hands on my abdomen, I felt my fear again, and had to caution her.

'You can't imagine how sensitive I feel there.'

'I'm not surprised,' she said, 'You've been kicked in the gut.'

Sometimes a simple sentence, even an old cliche, spoken at a moment of vulnerable opening, connects completely. Her statement immediately made it clear to me why I had colitis. I had colitis because I was living in a body filled with unrecognized rage.

I had loaned a woman I was crazy about money as we separated.

140

It was money I couldn't really afford to loan. Money she had promised to pay back at a specific date. The date had come and was now long gone.

'Have you heard from her?'

'Not a word.'

'Has she paid you anything back?'

'Nothing.'

The large, live animal I couldn't digest, the beast turning and churning in my gut, was my own unrecognized anger. I had been kicked in the guts by a woman with three inch heels, and I thought I was disappointed and saddened. What I really was, was enraged.

Some people have the idea that massage is a luxury for the very rich, a comfort of abundance that happens to tycoons who talk on the telephone while someone pounds on them like a baker making brioche. I blame it on the movies. In films massage is always nothing more than a part of the set. I don't normally think of myself as furniture.

I'm sometimes wrong about that, at least in my personal life, where I have been - at times - a footstool in a soap opera.

I had eaten my anger, and eating my anger had made my body bleed. The rage I was unable to acknowledge was threatening to blow up my belly like a paper thin tire on a sun-seared freeway. It was like winged scavengers with sharp beaks had been tearing at my entrails. I was metaphorically tied to the banks of my own alimentary canal by loyalty to a woman who didn't deserve loyalty.

This massage therapist had given me a gift beyond touch. Her presence and her massage opened me to the truth that I was angry. Now I could work toward venting that rage by finding a way to release it from my body, maybe get to the forgiveness that would eventually heal me.

Some body/mind tracts say colitis is "metaphysically" brought on by an overbearing mother. Every lover is also in many ways a mother to every man. Some say food equals love. If the body is annoyed by food, maybe that annoyance equals anger unrecognized. In other words, food taken into an angry body might sometimes cause the extreme internal irritation that we call colitis.

The colitis I experienced disappeared a month later on the third morning, of a three day fast. If the colon is inflamed by food, why not stop eating?

Surprising personal eurekas may explode more often than we know into the minds of the recumbent recipients of massage. Because massage is the closest thing to a meditative state that many will ever experience in this race for personal space which we call the modern world.

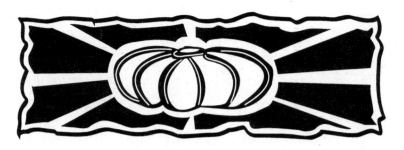

FLIGHT OF THE BEANBAGS

The MG sounded like an amplified bumblebee as we left Swiss Cottage going through the gears on the way out of London. I was catching a ride to the Isle of Wight with a friend who invited me to stay at her parents' place for several days with a group of friends. We were planning to attend a summer solstice celebration on the island.

The top was down, it was warm and I was trying to put a finger on the fragrance of London. It felt like home after four years and I loved it, but all I could come up with on this day was - a trace of mildew drying.

Much as I fed on it, the city sometimes seemed hard to me, like a week old hot cross bun. There was more brick here than anywhere I was sure, and the very cement of the sidewalks seemed older (and harder, I imagined) than the cement in other cities. Everything was ancient and loving and loving history, I was at home in the old world. The tiles in the Underground were older, the taxi cabs were older, the trains were older, the very dust seemed somehow older and the clothes too, and I was a whole lot younger.

Jill had invited me to a record release party Pink Floyd were giving several months before, for the 'Dark Side of the Moon' album. I couldn't remember much about the party, since before the party properly started, she enticed me into playing a game called 'shooters'. I lost too often, and shot so many shooters of scotch that I soon realized I was on my own dark side of the moon, located a comfortable place to lie down, and observed the shoes of various rock 'n' roll legends as they walked by my face on the floor.

We were soon off the motorway and bombing along a very zig zag English road on the Isle of Wight. The sun was out, the top was down, my hair was slapping my face. The overgrowth along the road was dense, not familiar to me and just high enough to completely limit visibility. I had an excited mysterious mind-set, a feeling of being driven into a labyrinth, and driving along it faster than comfort would allow.

I had long been impressed with English drivers, who cut their driving teeth on 'roundabouts', those circular junctions where as many as seven roads sometimes meet. Roundabouts are racing circles for some drivers, who jump down on the accelerator when they get to one, racing into the flow in order to achieve the exit road of choice before someone else already on the roundabout beats them to it. Jill's driving on the corkscrew roads she was familiar with was exhilarating and breathlessly so, since I didn't know the roads and couldn't see around the corners. I don't think she could either, but that didn't seem to bother her. For Jill, every corner was a chance to enjoy the gear-down, the acceleration, and the centrifugal force of cornering her screaming car.

As we neared our destination, she pointed down a country driveway where Elton John had a home. Several minutes later she was pulling off on a similar road and suddenly we drove into an English postcard. Before us was an ancestral English mansion, complete with circular driveway, and more rooms than could be taken in at a glance.

I was having some kind of trouble with a nerve pain in my hip. The pain caused me to squirm so much Jill thought I had been in mortal fear for my bones because of her daredevil driving. Which I sometimes was, I admit. I was awfully glad to get out of the car and stand in the magnificent courtyard, and finally be able to move about without a shooting pain coursing through my leg.

My pain was almost forgotten as we entered the receiving hall.

144

All around us, majestically surrounding the huge hall and larger than life, were oil portraits of six or seven hundred years of dead relatives. The dead relatives were so encrusted by the dust of the ages, and could only be seen dimly through the pale afternoon light. My mouth fell open as I gaped at the portraits. None of them were smiling, though I suppose sitting for portraits in their day, dead serious may have been the popular way to pose. The portraits were also hung along the great staircase to the second floor of the house, a floor I wistfully hoped I might achieve with Jill later on that night, though I never did get to climb the stairs.

Jill's father, 'The Colonel', showed me through the downstairs part of the house. Two English hunting dogs lying on hand-woven rugs worn thin by time, yawned as we walked though the main living room as though auditioning for parts in a Gothic Romance. The dinner table - not yet set for dining - was the longest I had ever seen. Jill's mother was welcoming, and eagerly mentioned awaiting her son 'a blue water sailor', who would arrive in his thirty eight foot yacht any day, having taken 'The Dingle Berry' to New York on a transatlantic race.

In California, a subdivision of thirty houses would have been developed on the estate, every driveway within fifty yards of the neighbor's driveway. Here, the empty tennis courts were only surrounded by copious bushes of various kinds in bloom. The green, wind-rippled lawn, dropped away like a smooth sail in a mild breeze to a cliff above the ocean.

The Colonel, before walking me down to overlook the view from the cliff, noticed I had a limp, and inquired after my health.

'Oh, just a pinched nerve,' I said.

'Just a pinched nerve! Good thing it isn't something serious, like pinched testicles.'

We were walking through the garden part of the lawn, and I was only a little surprised by his remark. England was a country of eccentrics, and although I had scant contact with the upper classes in my four years in London, it seemed to me like the more educated and upper class an Englishman was, the more eccentric he was likely to be.

'Well, the testicles are a little pinched too, Colonel. Bad case of Deadly Sperm Build-up.'

The Colonel let out a delighted, laughing harrumph.

'Better give you the old beanbag,' he said.

'Beanbag?'

'Didn't Jill tell you? I'm something of an amateur health enthusiast. Sort of a country healer. Better than being a completely professional health nut I suppose, like the Cracker Duchess next door, but I do specialize in South African beanbag treatments.'

'I've never heard of a beanbag treatment.'

'Simple stuff, really. A bag of sewn South African deer skin filled with Bumble Berries. Not even heavy. But bloody effective for the bum.'

'What's a Bumble Berry?'

'Haven't a clue, my dear. Just made it up. Have the damn things sent from Johannesburg. Probably full of beans. Probably why they call them beanbags, don't you think? Anyway, right through here ...' said the Colonel, opening a door to the stables.

In the stable house we were standing before bales of hay stacked high against a wall. A square of hay was zapped by a shaft of golden light streaming in through the window. The colonel showed me the beanbag he proposed to drop on me. He had me help him stack three bales of hay together and had me lie down on them on my stomach. Then he picked up the bean bag, which was like a bean filled beach-ball in a soiled, deerskin covering.

'Won't hurt a bit, my boy. Damn things are light as a feather,' he said, 'just relax..'

I was in a postcard in England with the landed gentry about to drop something huge on me, but I put my head down and attempted to relax.

Suddenly a smacking loud noise and a sensation of weight hit me and I could feel a rush of beans spread out across my buttocks; the initial impact followed by that brief and gentle settling of the beans, caused a blood rush of warmth.

'Hey, that felt good,' I said. 'Can you do it again?'

'Steady now. This is the Rhino Intestine Bean bag. Can you wiggle your left big toe?'

Another weight came crashing down on my backsides, flushing beans immediately saying hello to my tush as a thousand individual legumes.

The colonel had quite a sense of humor. After the 'Lion's Guts' bean bag hit my bottom, the 'Alligator Entrails' greeted my back, and the 'Elephant ears' bag 'of dried dung' landed on my derriere, I was, I have to admit, pretty relaxed. Of course, it was all the same bean bag, the variety of bag types only existed in his playful sense of humor. I felt somewhat better, but the nerve pain was still there.

The Colonel descended the crude, beam ladder.

'And now for the Pim's Cup,' he said. 'You'll be better in no time. Right as rain.'

'I'd rather be right as sunshine. But that was wonderful. Quite an amazing experience. Extraordinary the way it heats you up.'

'You let me know if it still hurts in an hour,' the Colonel said. 'I'll send you to the Cracker Duchess.'

'You mentioned her before. Why do you call her the Cracker Duchess?'

'Completely daffy neighbor. Not a Duchess, actually, and completely bats. We call her the Cracker Duchess because we once caught her driving her Mercedes over bags of crackers to crumble them. Didn't work very well; crackers all over the driveway. She's a brilliant Dame, really, as clever a duck as you'll ever meet. She flies down to Capetown from time to time to adjust circus elephants when their backs go out. Oh, she's way over the walk my boy, way over the walk, but she does know how to heal people.'

Even if my back had been healed by the flight of bean bags filled with God knows what I would have claimed pain, just to go 'way

147

over the walk' and meet the Duchess. As it turned out, 'way over the walk' was just a colloquialism for slightly bonkers. I didn't have to go to the Duchess; because the Duchess came to dinner. We were well into the after-dinner Port when the Colonel informed the Duchess that I was a 'pitiful human being with painfully constricted testicles and some kind of beanbag resistant, pinched nerve.'

'Oh my dear,' said the Duchess, 'we'll set you to rights on the dinner table after desert.'

'Not on my dinner table!' said the Lady of the house.

'I can't wait to see what you do for the testicles,' Jill teased.

'Well, ahhh, that was just a joke about the testicles,' I said.

'Said he had Deadly Sperm Build-up!' laughed the Colonel.

'I'm far too advanced to help you there, young man,' said the Duchess.

The ugly American was the after-dinner entertainment. I was instructed to 'gentle right down on the floor', where I was then twisted into an impossible pretzel position by the Duchess. Six people looked on, after-dinner port in their hands. The dogs were sniffing my parts. The Duchess wraps her arms around my neck, there's an incredibly loud snap, fireworks go off in my head, and waves of something begin rushing up my body and through the top of my head.

'Oh yes, seventh cervical was way out,' says the Duchess.

'What's happening to me?' I said, because I had never experienced such a sensation.

'What indeed?' inquired the Colonel.

'I don't know. Something's swimming up my body. I - I don't know. Can I look?'

'My God, it's the Silverfish,' said the Colonel, 'I knew it was time to clean the rugs.'

'Yes, let's have a look,' said the Duchess.

I lifted my shirt. Energy was rushing up my body, actually moving my flesh in waves.

'Look at that! Look at that! Can you see them?'

'Don't see a thing,' said the Colonel.

148

'The Kundalini,' said the Duchess.

'Does it hurt?' Jill asked.

'God, no. It feels magnificent! It's like I'm spewing electricity through the top of my head like a fountain.'

'This is very unusual,' said the Duchess. 'I've never seen this.'

'Whatever are you talking about?' Jill said.

'Oh, nevermind said the Duchess. But I will talk to you alone tomorrow young man.'

'Sure, oh thank you, thank you. I've never felt this way.'

'Most people never do,' she observed. 'I suggest you go outside and be alone for awhile.'

Outside, the sky was clear over the manicured landscape, the stars so brilliant I could see the various color variations in them, from yellow, through green to blue. The sensation of moving energy continued for nearly two hours. I couldn't sleep for excitement; and didn't want to sleep anyway.

The next day I followed Jill's directions up over a hill and through some trees on a path to the house where the Duchess lived. She was kneeling before some blackberry bushes with a spade, wearing a sun bonnet. When she saw me, she greeted me warmly, and rose to her feet. She was looking me over, but seemed to be looking beyond me. Finally, she smiled.

'What's wrong with your left eye?' she said.

'Oh, I had Bell's Palsy when I was a boy. The muscles have never returned to normal. It's pretty embarrassing when I get my picture taken.'

'You look like you have the mark of a healer.'

'Meaning what?'

'Hard to explain, exactly. The open eye. The inward looking eye. Every primitive tribe knows it. You have no idea what I'm talking about?'

'No.'

'And you don't know what happened last night?'

'Well, you made me feel fantastic. And my hip doesn't hurt to-

149

day.'

'People try for years to experience what happened to you last night. Have you ever fallen hard on your head?'

'Yes, I did fall off a swing on to some cement once.'

'Migraine headaches?'

'I did have migraines until I was seventeen. Then they stopped.'

'Psychic experiences?'

'Some pretty strange ones.'

'Well, you might consider looking into the healing arts. Take meditation classes. Study yoga. Read up on Ayurvedic medicine. Read everything esoteric. Find out about auras. Look into every kind of body/mind book you can come across. You'll find it very interesting.'

'Why?'

'There are energies in the body that can get released and overwhelm people. I don't know why, but you seem to be one of those people. I know, because I am too. People think I'm weird.'

'People always tell me I'm weird. They don't mean anything by it. They just mean I'm different.'

'You are different. But if you don't find out how you're different it could drive you 'round the bend.'

At the time, I didn't take her too seriously. After getting into massage, I took it all very seriously, maybe too seriously sometimes. I'll always enjoy giving massage, but I don't try to fix anybody anymore. I'm inclined to think anybody in the healing professions is akin to an ironic, fragile mirror. We're all trying to heal our own wounds by attempting to touch reflections of ourselves that appear before us as other people. It may even be that we need to touch others because we too often feel, in some essential way, out of touch in the world.

The Isle of Wight was soon no more than a fading memory among many English memories, and I soon forgot the Duchess of Crackers.

MICHAEL WINECOFF

HAS BEEN A LICENSED MASSAGE THERAPIST
FOR 16 YEARS. MICHAEL WROTE THE COLUMN
'INTERACTIONS' FOR MASSAGE MAGAZINE, WAS
THE FOUNDER/DIRECTOR OF THE GATEWAY
ATHLETIC CLUB MASSAGE PROGRAM IN SEATTLE,
HAS WRITTEN A MOVIE REVIEW COLUMN & HAD
FICTION, NON-FICTION & POEMS PUBLISHED IN
THE USA & ENGLAND. THE COVER ART FOR
HANDS-ON HEART WAS SUGGESTED IN A
DRAWING BY MARIAH LAUTHNER, AGE 7.

Assorted Moments With :

"Poor dogs," I said when I removed her ballet
shoes and saw her mangled feet.
"Poor dogs," she echoed, though I wasn't sure she
knew enough English to understand what it meant.
Russian Ballerina

"Go easy on my back. I've still got some schrapnel
in it from the Korean war."
Hollywood Screen Star

"If you would rather read the paper than have the
massage," I said, I can wait 'till you're finished with
it,"
"No, I'll read it later. It's an article about me, so
I was anxious to look at it."
NBA team President, when he was
a player for a club he now runs.

"We're all wrecked. The floor in Oakland isn't a
'sprung' floor and it always kills us."
New York City ballet
dancer in pain.

"You should have a drool pan located under this
table."
"Don't quote me"

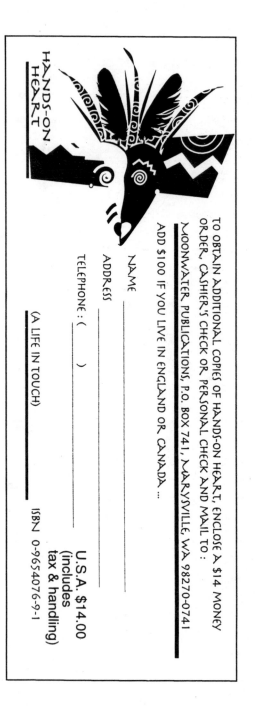

HANDS-ON HEART

TO OBTAIN ADDITIONAL COPIES OF HANDS-ON HEART, ENCLOSE A $14 MONEY
ORDER, CASHIER'S CHECK OR PERSONAL CHECK AND MAIL TO :

MOONWATER PUBLICATIONS, P.O. BOX 741, MARYSVILLE, WA. 98270-0741

ADD $100 IF YOU LIVE IN ENGLAND OR CANADA ...

NAME

ADDRESS

TELEPHONE : (   )

(A LIFE IN TOUCH)

ISBN 0-9654076-9-1

U.S.A. $14.00
(includes
tax & handling)

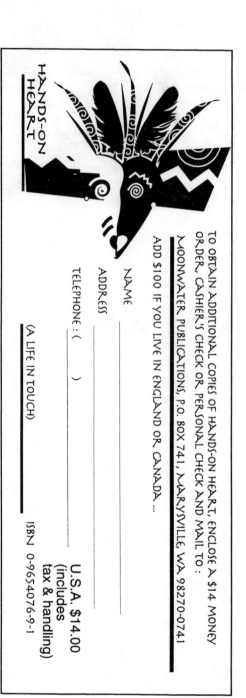

HANDS-ON HEART

TO OBTAIN ADDITIONAL COPIES OF HANDS-ON HEART, ENCLOSE A $14 MONEY ORDER, CASHIER'S CHECK OR PERSONAL CHECK AND MAIL TO :

MOONWATER PUBLICATIONS, P.O. BOX 741, MARYSVILLE, WA 98270-0741

ADD $100 IF YOU LIVE IN ENGLAND OR CANADA ...

NAME _____

ADDRESS _____

TELEPHONE : ( ) _____

(A LIFE IN TOUCH)

ISBN 0-9654076-9-1

U.S.A. $14.00
(includes
tax & handling)